Respublica

EARLY ENGLISH TEXT SOCIETY

Original Series No. 226

1952 (for 1946), reprinted 1969

PRICE 30s.

Respublica

An interlude for Christmas 1553

attributed to

NICHOLAS UDALL

RE-EDITED BY
W. W. GREG

Published for
THE EARLY ENGLISH TEXT SOCIETY
by the
OXFORD UNIVERSITY PRESS
LONDON   NEW YORK   TORONTO

OXFORD
UNIVERSITY PRESS

Great Clarendon Street, Oxford OX2 6DP
United Kingdom

Oxford University Press is a department of the University of Oxford.
It furthers the University's objective of excellence in research, scholarship,
and education by publishing worldwide. Oxford is a registered trade mark of
Oxford University Press in the UK and in certain other countries

© The Early English Text Society 1952

The moral rights of the authors have been asserted

Database right Oxford University Press (maker)

First Edition published in 1952
Reprinted 1969

All rights reserved. No part of this publication may be reproduced,
stored in a retrieval system, or transmitted, in any form or by any means,
without the prior permission in writing of Oxford University Press,
or as expressly permitted by law, or under terms agreed with the appropriate
reprographics rights organization. Enquiries concerning reproduction
outside the scope of the above should be sent to the Rights Department,
Oxford University Press, at the address above

You must not circulate this book in any other form
and you must impose this same condition on any acquirer

Published in the United States of America by Oxford University Press
198 Madison Avenue, New York, NY 10016, United States of America

British Library Cataloguing in Publication Data
Data available

Library of Congress Cataloging in Publication Data
Data available

Original Series, 226

ISBN 978-0-19-722226-3

CONTENTS

INTRODUCTION
  The Manuscript and the Editions   vii
  Authorship   viii
  The Writing of the Manuscript and its Treatment in the Present Edition   xviii

TEXT   1

GLOSSARY   67

INTRODUCTION

The Manuscript and the Editions

THE Macro manuscript of *Respublica* has already been printed four times: by J. P. Collier as the third item in the first volume of his *Illustrations of Old English Literature*, 1866; by Alois Brandl in his *Quellen des weltlichen Dramas in England*, 1898 (pp. 281–358); by L. A. Magnus for the Early English Text Society in 1905 (Extra Series, xciv); and, modernized, by J. S. Farmer in his *Recently Recovered 'Lost' Tudor Plays with Some Others*, 1907 (pp. 177–272). Farmer also issued a collotype facsimile (by Fleming) in 1908. The editions by Brandl and Magnus contain some intelligent emendations along with a number of serious mistakes and a host of minor errors. The errors are less excusable in the case of Magnus, seeing that he had Brandl's text for comparison.

The manuscript once belonged to the famous antiquary Sir Henry Spelman (1564?–1641) and early in the eighteenth century passed into the hands of another well-known collector, the Rev. Cox Macro (1683–1767) of Little Haugh, Norton, Suffolk. Macro's library came into the possession of John Pattenson, M.P. for Norwich, and was sold at Christie's in 1820. On this occasion the *Respublica* manuscript, together with that of the so-called 'Macro Moralities', was acquired by Hudson Gurney (1775–1864) of Keswick Hall, Norfolk, and they remained in his family till the Gurney sale at Sotheby's on 30 March 1936, when the Moralities passed (through Quaritch) to the Folger Shakespeare Library, Washington, and *Respublica* into the possession of Mr. Carl H. Pforzheimer of New York.[1]

As appears from the foliation, which runs from 360 to 387, the twenty-eight leaves of the manuscript once formed part of a larger volume. It appears to have been preceded by a copy of the *Glossarium originale de Iohannis de Laet*, and to have been followed by antiquarian collections, copies of charters and the like, presumably gathered by Spelman, which are now in the Public Library

---

[1] See the *Pforzheimer Catalogue*, 1940, ii. 531–2, from which most of the particulars regarding the manuscript are, by permission, taken. I am also indebted to the kindness of Mr. Pforzheimer and his librarian, Miss Emma Va. Unger, for information respecting a number of readings in the manuscript that the facsimile leaves in doubt.

at Norwich. The interlude was separately bound for Collier's use in 1836. It appears to be written on five quires in folio (measuring 11½ by 8 inches), the first and fourth of eight leaves and the rest of four. This collation is based on the recurrence of the watermark, which closely resembles Briquet's no. 11378, a design found from 1548 to 1569. The manuscript itself bears the date 1553, but this is given as that of composition, so that the actual writing may be later. A worm has eaten its way throughout the leaves, but its depredations are only serious towards the end. The catalogue describes them as 'in the inner margins', but it is in fact the text that has suffered.

Authorship

In the Introduction to his edition of *Respublica* Magnus drew attention to several important documents among the Loseley manuscripts which may have a bearing upon the production and authorship of the play. He relied upon the catalogue by A. J. Kempe (*Manuscripts preserved in the Muniment Room at Loseley House*, 1835), but the documents have since been more fully and reliably edited by Albert Feuillerat (*Documents relating to the Revels at Court in the time of King Edward VI and Queen Mary*, Louvain, 1914), and we are therefore in a slightly better position than was Magnus to assess the exact value of their evidence.

The crucial document is a warrant addressed by the Queen to the officers of the Revels dated 13 December 'in the Seconde yere of our Reigne', i.e. 1554, authorizing the delivery of playing apparel to Nicholas Udall, who 'haith at sondry seasons convenient hertofore shewid and myndeth herafter to shewe his diligence in settinge forthe of dialogwes and Entreludes before vs for our Regall disport and recreacion' (Feuillerat, p. 159). From this we are bound to conclude that by early December 1554, that is before the Christmas season, Udall had already produced at least one play at court before the Queen.[1] *Respublica* appears to be such a play, and it is therefore conceivable that it was Udall's. Of course there may have been other court dramatists besides Udall, and

[1] The words 'sondry seasons' suggest more than one, but, as we shall see in a moment, they may imply diversity of occasion rather than of composition. Alternatively he may have written masques, for instance the All-Hallows Masque of Mariners in 1554 (Feuillerat, p. 161).

INTRODUCTION ix

were there evidence that a number of plays had been acted at court in the first year of Mary's reign, the reason for connecting *Respublica* with Udall would be slight. But in fact, apart from a masque or two, it appears highly improbable that more than one (or at most two) dramatic entertainments had been given. The claim of *Respublica* to have been that piece deserves in consequence closer attention.

Now we know from another warrant issued to the Revels Office on 26 September 'the fyrste yeare of owr reigne', i.e. 1553, that a play or interlude had been prepared by the gentlemen (or children) of the Chapel Royal in connexion with the Queen's coronation on 1 October, but that it was for some reason postponed till Christmas (Feuillerat, p. 149; cf. p. 150, line 9). *Respublica* does not indeed mention Mary's coronation, but her accession is clearly related to the happy outcome of the action; it is a Christmas play (l. 6) performed by a company of children (ll. 39 ff.); the ending suggests, though it does not necessarily imply, that it was given at court; and the heading states that it was made in 1553, 'the first yeare of the moost prosperous Reigne of our moste gracious Soveraigne Quene Marye the first'. This fits in well enough with its being the play prepared for the coronation and postponed to Christmas.[1]

The only objection to this obvious conclusion is the existence of another warrant from the Queen, this time to the Master of the Great Wardrobe, dated 30 September 'in the first yere of oure Reigne', i.e. four days after the one already mentioned. It is for the provision of material for costumes also 'for the gentlemen of oure chapell for a play to be playde before vs for the feastes of oure coronacion', and it names a number of the characters appearing,

[1] Recording the postponement Magnus remarks (p. xvii) that this 'obliges us to suppose that the Respublica was intended, for Christmas 1553, but postponed'. One would suppose that this was a mere slip were it not for his later remark (p. xxi): 'If, as we have seen, the Coronation play was deferred to Christmas 1553, this must have been longer postponed; and this would explain' the lines, *Resp.* 1934–5,

Praying that hir Reigne mooste graciouslye begonne
Maie long yeares endure as hithertoo yt hath doone.

This certainly looks at first as though the reign had already lasted some years: the meaning, however, is, may it last long as prosperously as it has begun. There is no reason whatever to suppose that *Respublica* was not acted, as it claims to have been written, for Mary's first Christmas.

namely Genus Humanum, Reason, Verity, Plenty, Selflove, Care, Scarcity, Deceit, Sickness, Feebleness, Deformity, five virgins, and an epilogue (Feuillerat, p. 289, from the Exchequer Accounts in P.R.O.). Now, though the theme may have been similar, this play was obviously not *Respublica*, and if, as Feuillerat evidently did, we identify this coronation play with the one postponed to Christmas, then the proposed identification of the latter with *Respublica* falls to the ground. But there does not appear to be any conclusive reason why the two coronation plays should be the same. May not *Genus Humanum* be the play in favour of which *Respublica* was deferred till Christmas? Indeed, one document records the charges incurred between 22 September 1553 and 6 January following 'to furnysshe owte certen playes settfoorth by the gentilmen of the Chapell' (Feuillerat, p. 290). Feuillerat, it is true, declares this to be an error, since 'the accounts and the docquets prove beyond doubt that only one play was performed'. One hesitates to differ from so experienced an archivist and expert a scholar as Feuillerat, who moreover had all the documents before him, but I fail to see that his conclusion necessarily follows from those that he has printed. If he is right, and only one play was performed at court in the first year of Mary's reign,[1] we are driven to the conclusion that Udall was the author of *Genus Humanum*, and that *Respublica*, though written for Christmas 1553, was either not acted, or was not intended for court performance.

This is as far as the external evidence will take us, and any further attempt to connect *Respublica* with Udall must be based on internal criteria. Magnus drew attention to what he called 'some curious results' of a comparison of *Respublica* with *Roister Doister*, a play that Udall is known to have written shortly before the date in question; and he also collected a number of verbal parallels, though by no means all or even the most significant. It may also be remarked that in a brief article in *Modern Language Notes* in 1927 (xlii. 378–80) Leicester Bradner of Brown University pointed out a remarkable likeness of metrical structure between the two plays, and though it is perhaps not altogether easy

---

[1] In that case the scribe of the document was presumably misled by the fact that expenses had been incurred both in the preparation of a play for the coronation and in the production of a play at Christmas, although in fact only one piece was involved.

INTRODUCTION xi

to assess the value of the evidence, the figures he was able to quote are certainly striking.

One point of resemblance that must strike even the most casual reader is the naivety of the devices used for getting the characters onto the stage. There is, of course, nothing unusual about this in the crude dramaturgy of the early stage, but the frequency of what might be called the *lupus in fabula* formula (see *Respublica*, 749) becomes almost monotonous. It is well illustrated by the first instance in *Roister Doister* (66):

> I wyll seeke him out: But loe he commeth thys way,

others may be found at 781, 888, and 1327. In *Respublica* the same formula is used at 154, 532, 609, 634, 749, 825, 984, 998, 1206, 1338, 1394, 1482, and 1613. A similar frankness appears in the formula with which the prologue leaves the stage: *Respublica*, 57:

> Nowe yf yowe so please, I wyll goe,

Roister Doister, Prol. 29:

> And here I take my leaue for a certaine space.

Another noticeable feature is the fondness for dragging in songs, usually to close a scene; for example in *Roister Doister* at 253, 303, 515, 536, and 690, and in *Respublica* at 123, 597, 1430, 1660, and 1939.

One of the most curious features of the verse in *Respublica* is the repetition of the same word in place of a rhyme, sometimes for several lines together, as in 478 ff., where seven consecutive lines end with the word 'Policy' in a nice variety of spellings. The same habit may be observed in *Roister Doister* at 149–50, 173–4, 203–4, 588–9, 668–9, 1398–9, 1406–7, 1416–17, 1698–9, 1741–2, 1844–5, while the six lines 396–401 end uniformly with 'Een so sir'.

Incidentally it may be mentioned that when in *Roister Doister* (362–3) Madge Mumblecrust, for no apparent reason, lapses into dialect, it is the dialect spoken by People in *Respublica*—

> God yelde you sir, chad not so much ichotte not whan,
> Nere since chwas bore chwine, of such a gay gentleman—

and that Dobinet Doughty mauls a Latin tag, 'Nobs nicebecetur miserere' (419), just as People does 'diuum este, Iusllum weste' (1090). Mention of these characters recalls the consistent alliteration of the names in *Roister Doister*, not only of the personae but of a series of imaginary characters in 19–27: there was, of course, no place for such fireworks in the more serious characters of *Respublica*, but we may note the passing allusions to 'Iohn lacke latten' (959), 'Piers Piekpurse' (1246), as well as the 'prioure of Prickingham' (884).

A fondness for proverbs and for quasi-proverbial expressions, sometimes introduced by 'they say' or some such phrase (*Resp.* 116, 749; *R.D.* 81), manifests itself in both plays, as indeed in some others. In *Roister Doister* we find instances at 81, 270-1, 273, 873, 985, and 1815; in *Respublica* at 116, 117, 262, 287-8, 674, 796, 1014, 1120, 1322, 1443, and 1587. But among so many there is little repetition: only one, I think, is common to the two pieces. In *Respublica* (946) we have:

> to take flyght or anie grasse, maie growe on hir hele

and in *Roister Doister* (1031):

> There hath grown no grasse on my heele since I went hence,

and (1513):

> since I went no grasse hath growne on my hele ...

Another pair of phrases is, however, worth recalling, namely, *Respublica*, 1033:

> Nowe by the compace that god coumpaced

and *Roister Doister*, 622:

> Nowe by the token that God tokened

'compace' and 'token' being, of course, caught up from what has gone before.

There is an obvious parallel between *Respublica*, 1701-3:

> welcome faire Ladie swete ladie, litle ladye,
> plaine ladie, smoothe ladie, somey, me spittle ladye,
> Ladie longtong, ladye tell all, ladie make bate

and *Roister Doister*, 1420-3:

> Gentle mistresse Custance now, good mistresse Custance,
> Honey mistresse Custance now, sweete mistresse Custance,
> Golden mistresse Custance now, white mistresse Custance,
> Silken mistresse Custance now, faire mistresse Custance.

Even more remarkable is the passing and rather obscure allusion to the removing of a speck of dust from Respublica's gown (564-5):

> By your lycence madame to take awaie this mote.—
> Naie honestie will not see a wemme on your Cote

INTRODUCTION xiii

a piece of business that is developed at length in *Roister Doister* (502-9):

> By your maisterships licence.—What is that? a moate?—
> No it was a fooles feather had light on your coate.—
> I was nigh no feathers since I came from my bed.—
> No sir, it was a haire that was fall from your hed.—
> . . . .—By your leue.—What is that?—
> Your gown was foule spotted with the foot of a gnat.—. . .
> What now?—A lousy haire from your masterships beard.

From these more general likenesses we may pass to those of vocabulary and verbal usage, some of which are among the most striking of all. And here we may cast our net rather wider to include, besides the two plays, two of Udall's translations, namely, *Apophthegms first gathered by Erasmus*, 1542 (containing the third and fourth books of the original work), and *The first tome of the Paraphrase of Erasmus upon the New Testament*, by Udall and others, 1548 (Udall being, it seems, in particular responsible for Luke).[1]

The following are, I think, the most striking parallels.

There is a rare use of the adv. *since* with the force of 'already, now', for which the only quotations in *O.E.D.* are two passages from *R.D.*

> 342 Haue we done singyng since? then will I in againe
> 1195 But lo and Merygreeke haue not brought him sens?

to which may be added

> 1030 But lo, how well Merygreeke is returned sence.

This use is common in *Resp.*, e.g.

> 1730 Somes teeth I thinke water een sens to bee snatching

---

[1] For *Roister Doister* I have used the Malone Society's reprint of the imperfect original of ?1566. For references to the *Apophthegms* and the *Paraphrase* I am dependent on the *Oxford English Dictionary*. There are, of course, several other acknowledged works of Udall's, but I have not noticed any significant quotations from them in *O.E.D.* When citing *O.E.D.* as evidence for the rarity of certain words, I am of course fully aware that its collections are far from exhaustive for the sixteenth century, especially in the earlier volumes. The extent to which this deficiency invalidates any deductions made on the basis of that evidence has been impressed on me, not for the first time, by Professor F. P. Wilson, who very obligingly read this section in manuscript, and who has allowed me to incorporate into it some valuable notes he communicated. Nevertheless he agrees that there is a strong case for Udall's authorship. Incidentally he mentions that the uses of the proverbial phrases about grass growing on the heels and bees in the brain are the earliest he has come across.

also 260, 319, 532, 763, 1599. Professor F. P. Wilson has drawn my attention to a somewhat similar use in Gascoigne's *Supposes*, I. ii. 92:

> Why, euen now, I came but from thence since

(i.e. immediately).

Then there is the word *rahated* in *Resp.* 364:

> and is not flaterie openly rahated?

which has puzzled editors, who have either misread it as, or emended it to, *rabated*. *O.E.D.*, however, gives it as a variant of *rated*, scolded, quoting as the only examples *Apoph.*

> 77[b] He neuer lynned rahatyng those persones
> 84[b] To bee chidden and rahated of all the worlde.

There is a curious phrase that appears twice in *Resp.*

> 276 Than must ye looke a lofte with handes vnder the side
> 1796 than pranketh she hir elbowse owte vnder hir side

I do not know what it means, but it is also found in *R.D.*

> 1001 That is a lustie brute, handes vnder your side man

At *Resp.* 1044 People's *of zemlitee* seems to mean 'to all appearance' (cf. 1242 *of likelihood*); *zemlitee* being a perversion of *semblety*, itself a nonce-formation from the adj. *semble*, like or resembling. In *R.D.* we actually find:

> 482 A sore man by zembletee

(i.e. 'so it seems') spoken by Madge, who, as we have already seen, lapses on occasion into People's dialect.

At *Resp.* 340 we find mention of 'myne owne good spaignell Rigg', and again at *R.D.* 682 'like our spaniell Rig'. The phrase does not appear to be proverbial and has a personal ring. But Rig was an accepted name for a dog, and as such appears in Ulpian Fulwell's *Ars Adulandi*, 1576 (sig. G3).

In *Resp.* 1804 *aprehende* means to arrest or hold in custody. The only sixteenth-century quotation for this legal sense in *O.E.D.* is from *Paraph.* John, vii. 1, 'to attache and apprehende him'. But it must have been current. Dogberry's perversion 'comprehend all vagrom men', *Much Ado*, III. iii. 25–6, proves that the use was familiar enough by the end of the century.

The word *elf* in the sense of an imp, a mischievous person, occurs in *Resp.* at 259, 1011, and 1831. The only sixteenth-century quota-

INTRODUCTION

tion for this meaning in *O.E.D.* is *R.D.* 956, 'these women be all such madde pieuishe elues'.

At *Resp.* 441 we meet with the phrase 'from so florent estate', i.e. from such a flourishing condition. The word *florent* may not strike us as particularly out of the way, but in fact the only quotation for it in *O.E.D.*, apart from two eighteenth-century instances from Durfey, is *Apoph.* 68^b, 'Sinopa . . . was a florent citee'.

At *Resp.* 180 is the word *iacke* for fellow, knave; and the only quotation in *O.E.D.* for this sense before Shakespeare is *Paraph.* Luke vi. 65, 'that euery iacke vseth'. The word, however, has the same meaning, worthless fellow, in *The Book of Merchants*, ed. 1547, sig. f5^v, and was probably common.

At *Resp.* 1900 *pardon* is found in the sense of leave, permission:

Leat me than with pardon goe hens abowte yt lightlye.

Apart from Shakespeare, *O.E.D.* has only one quotation for this meaning, namely, *Paraph.* Acts, xxvi. 84, 'Thou haste pardon to speake for thy selfe'.

In *shuttle brained* at *Resp.* 1293, *shuttle* is a variant of *shittle*, unsteady (cf. People's *skittlebraine*, 1811, 1817). The only other sixteenth-century quotation for the form in *O.E.D.* is from *Apoph.* 307^b, 'Metellus was so shuttlebrained'; but it is also found in Barnaby Rich's *Don Simonides*, 1581, sig. A4.

At *Resp.* 1703 occurs the phrase 'to take . . . in a tryppe', that is to catch tripping, to detect in an error, but *O.E.D.* suggests that it may have been misunderstood to mean 'to take in a trap' (a form actually found at 1612): the phrase is used in exactly the same way in *Paraph.* Mark, x. 63, 'desired more to take him in a trip', and also in Udall's *Flowers for Latin Speaking*, 1533 (ed. 1560, sig. I7). But it also occurs in Thomas Wilson's *Discourse upon Usury*, 1572 (ed. 1925, p. 180).

Whatever deductions have to be made for the imperfection of the records, the significance of these parallels will hardly be disputed. Some others, less distinctive, may be added.

abusion, abuse, deceit, 24: cf. *Paraph.*, preface to Mark, 'false doctrine, the roote and chief cause of all abusions'.

armes, 'by his armes', 128, also 'by his woundes', 130: cf. *R.D.* 576, 'his armes and woundes', and 977, 'Armes what dost thou?'

armes of Callis, 782: cf. *R.D.* 1110, 1663, 'the armes of Caleys'. The expression is also in Skelton.

B

INTRODUCTION

bees, 'I have a hive of humble bees swarmynge in my braine', 66: cf. *R.D.* 500, 'Who so hath suche bees as your maister in hys head'.

breake, put an end to, 167, 1228: cf. *R.D.* 1491, 'Will ye my tale breake?'

cockes, 'cockes bones', 949; 'cockes passion', 1867: cf. *R.D.* 430, 'Kocks nownes'; 230, 'By cocke'; 290, 'By Cock'.

coilled, beaten, 1811: cf. *R.D.* 1466-7, 'I shall cloute thee . . . And coyle thee'; *Apoph.* 7^b, 'more neede of coiling'; and *Paraph.* Luke xx. 159^a, 'When they had sore coyled him'.

commontie, commonality, *Dram. Pers.*: cf. *R.D.* 2006, 'With all the whole commontie'.

frame, to shape, prosper, 'howe dyd all frame', 821; 'I tolde you ever . . . that your welth woulde frame', 1331: cf. *R.D.* 256, 'My matter frameth well'; 280, 'this geare beginneth for to frame'.

gawdes, objects of mockery, sport, 1651: cf. *R.D.* 1039, 'gaudyng and foolyng'.

gentman, 1068; *ientman*, 1006, 1031: cf. *R.D.* 2059, 'gentman'; 904, 1198, 'ientman'.

gosse, 'by gosse', 315: cf. *R.D.* 1129, 'By gosse': *gos* is properly a possessive, standing for 'God's', as in the phrase 'gos bones'.

grownde, a particular spot of land, 828: cf. *Paraph.* Matt. xxvii. 7, 'they bought a ground of a certayne potter'.

grutche, an earlier form of 'grudge', is frequent for complaint, resentment, 214 &c., and also occurs as a verb, 799: the verb is in *R.D.* 1523.

houghe as a spelling of 'ho!' is at 898 S.D.: cf. *R.D.* 78, 380, 'hough'.

ichill ieoperde a ioincte, I will risk a limb, 1606: cf. *R.D.* 1752, 'I durst ieoparde my hande'.

ka, quoth, 1031, 1043: cf. *R.D.* 181, 'Enamoured ka?': *O.E.D.* has only two quotations: the more usual 'ko' is in *R.D.* 904-5 and 918-20.

lo, loe, to look, 1165, 1219; cf. *R.D.* 998, 'so loe, vp man' (where the comma is an error); 999, 'so loe, nowe ye begin'.

malkin, a woman, 644: cf. *R.D.* 184.

masship, mastership, 813, 841, 1053: cf. *R.D.* 170, 186, 440, &c.

mome, dolt, 348: cf. *R.D.* 869, 1852, 1925.

INTRODUCTION xvii

nowe of daies, a rather uncommon variant, 1431: cf. *Apoph*. 223, 'Such as our princes & noble menne haue nowe of dayes'.

pashe of god, 1645, 1907: cf. *R.D.* 1470, 'for the paishe of God'; 1665, 1921, 'for the pashe of God'; 1788, 'for the pashe of our sweete Lord'.

passe, issue, end, 1854: cf. *Apoph*. 1. *Socr*. § 93 n., 38ᵃ, 'bryng the same ... to such passe and effecte, as he would dooe'.

paules steeple, 635; *polle steple*, 1010: cf. *R.D.* 761, 'out of the toppe of Paules steeple'.

polle, to plunder, rob, 843: cf. *R.D.* 1216 'by polling and bribes'.

rag of rhetorike, 919: cf. *R.D.* 1427, 'a ragge of your Rhetorike'.

rather, earlier, 'later or rather', 197; cf. *R.D.* 1207, 'later or rather'.

Saincte George the borowe, 579: cf. *R.D.* 1689, 1781, 'sainct George to borow'.

sectourshipp, executorship, 863, 865: cf. *R.D.* 945, 'Thou shalt be my sectour'. The proper form is 'secutor', though 'sector' is not uncommon.

shake up, 'Thei shaked me vp, chwas ner zo rattled avore', 1586: cf. *R.D.* 612, 'I was nere so shoke vp afore'.

shrewe, beshrew, curse, 'I shrewe his naked harte', 1303: cf. *R.D.* 306, 'I shrew them'; 870, 'I shrew his head'; 1343, 'I shrew their best ... chekes'; 1912, 'I shrewe his best cheeke'.

spill, to destroy, 1859: cf. *R.D.* 1692.

staighe, a spelling of *stay*, 457, 735: cf. *Apoph*. preface, 'our whole trust and staigh'.

starke, sheer, very, 'starke bedlems', 1112; cf. *R.D.* 264, 'starke nyght'.

swim, to move smoothly, 'as he swymmed or glided vppon yce', 1275: cf. *R.D.* 681, 'ye shall see hir glide and swimme'.

then, however, on the other hand (more usually 'but then'), 'Than have ye whole townes', 834: 'Then mercye ys a goode one', 1465; cf. *R.D.* 861, 'He shall neuer haue me hys wife while he doe liue.—Then will he haue you if he may'.

waste, 'in waste', in vain, 1442: cf. *R.D.* 1403, 'his labour hither he shall spende in wast'; 1525, 'ye shall not sende in wast'.

what, exclamation, 'And what are yowe nowe in any goode hope to thryve?' 779: cf. *R.D.* 231, 'What if Christian Custance will not haue you what?'

whoughe, how!, 721: cf. *R.D.* 527, 'Whough, dost thou doubt of that?' and *Apoph.* 314, 'Whough, saieth he, half my brothers bodye is more then the whole'.

zelosie, zelousye, meaning mistrust, 995, 1770, is a rare formation from the adj. 'zealous', perhaps confused with 'jealous', but it is found in *Apoph.* 11. 117^b, 'the zelousie, and eagre feersnes of Olympias'.

The value of parallels as evidence of common authorship is notoriously uncertain, and many of the similarities cited above would of course be wholly without significance taken by themselves. There are others, however, whose pertinence is beyond question, and taken as a whole I feel that they point sufficiently clearly to a single author to justify placing Udall's name on the title of the present edition. It should be added that the manuscript is not in Udall's handwriting;[1] but neither, to judge from the nature of the errors, does it seem likely to be autograph.

The Writing of the Manuscript and its Treatment in the Present Edition

The text of the present edition is based on that already published by the Early English Text Society in 1905, but this has been repeatedly collated with the facsimile and also with Brandl's edition.

The manuscript is written in a very clear mid-sixteenth-century hand using both secretary and Italian scripts, which are, as a rule, clearly distinguished, except in some of the Latin directions, which though fundamentally secretary, show an Italian admixture. Pure Italian appears only in certain (by no means all) Latin phrases and a few proper names in the text. The speeches are usually divided by rules running across the page, with the speaker's prefix opposite the beginning of the rule rather than the first line of the speech. Passages, however, in which the speakers alternate quickly, and in which some of the prefixes are therefore placed within the line, are generally treated as verse paragraphs with rules only at the beginning and the end.[2]

---

[1] See *English Literary Autographs, 1550–1650*, part ii, plate XXXII (1928). I there spoke guardedly about the attribution of *Respublica*, but I had not at the time studied the evidence in detail.

[2] The pages were evidently ruled with speech-lines before the text was

INTRODUCTION xix

For the sake of distinction act and scene headings, together with the character lists at the beginning of the scenes, and speakers' prefixes, have been printed in italic, although they are in secretary script in the original. Similarly stage directions have been italicized whatever the script used in the manuscript. Otherwise the original has been carefully followed, secretary being represented by roman type and Italian script by italic.

Italic has also been used to expand contractions of the original writing. But it has only been used to replace conventional signs and to supply omitted letters: superior letters that retain their habitual form are printed in roman. (In the case of words printed in italic, contractions are, of course, expanded in roman.) There are, however, in the original many flourishes and seeming contraction-marks that appear to be without significance: these have been ignored even in cases in which it would be possible to give them a meaning. For example, the common termination '-on' is always written with a curl above it, and it would be quite reasonable to render it by '-ou*n*', were it not that the preposition is written in exactly the same way. It has been the rule, therefore, to ignore all would-be contraction-marks that are not essential.

The usually rather scanty punctuation of the manuscript has been, as a rule, retained, and only such points as appeared necessary to the understanding of the text have been (silently) added. Points have been supplied when needed after speakers' names and stage directions and at the end of speeches. But points are not always reproduced exactly as in the original. In this commas (small semicircles) and periods (mere dots) are both common and are clearly distinguished in shape, but they are used quite indiscriminately, and in printing it has therefore been necessary to differentiate them, not according to shape, but according to the sense of the passage. (I get the impression that the dots alone belong to the original writing, and that the commas, which occur almost exclusively within the line, were added by the scribe on reading through the text, together with

written, and occasionally insufficient space was left between them: see footnotes to ll. 194–6, 208–9, and 1554–5. The method appears most clearly at ll. 787–92. Here space for six lines was quite correctly left blank between the rules; but the scribe made an error that necessitated his cancelling the second line he wrote, with the result that the last five lines had to be crowded into the space left for four.

the comparatively rare colons and semicolons.) Question-marks are fairly frequent. (They, too, are almost certainly later additions since they have repeatedly been added to the wrong one of two adjacent lines and sometimes appear superimposed on other stops.) But they are by no means always used correctly. Many interrogative sentences lack them, and they occur not seldom where they are not wanted. In the latter case they may possibly sometimes stand for marks of exclamation, but they are more probably mere errors and have been so treated. One apparent exclamation-mark appears, at l. 1336. In printing, question-marks have been supplied where needed and omitted where not required; but both insertion and omission have been recorded in the footnotes. Virgules (sloping strokes) are fairly common: where they occur alone they have been retained, where in addition to other punctuation marks they have been ignored.

Though the writing is very clear it yet presents a few difficulties to the transcriber. For one thing 'n' and 'u' are indistinguishable in shape and have to be distinguished by the sense, which is occasionally ambiguous. Less important, but more troublesome, is the difficulty of distinguishing between majuscule and minuscule forms at the beginning of words, where they are used with something approaching indifference. In the case of some letters the forms are quite distinct (e.g. B, C, T), and when this is so I have followed the original scrupulously. In others the forms pass into one another insensibly (e.g. D, M, W). In cases of uncertainty I have allowed capitals to proper names (and generally at the beginning of speeches and lines) but not elsewhere. I have retained the sometimes erratic word-division of the original, even though it may now and then present difficulties to the reader. It would in any case be hard to determine the author's real intention, especially in the artificial dialect spoken by People, and once start interfering with what the scribe has written, or appears to have written, and it is impossible to know where to stop. If 'cannot' is one word, why not 'donot' as well? 'wilbe' and 'shalbe' are recognized forms, and it is clear that to the scribe at least 'orels' was just as much one word as 'into'.

Mutilations are indicated by pointed brackets, within which are printed all damaged letters that are in any degree doubtful. Thus the restorations that appear between such brackets must be

INTRODUCTION   xxi

treated as conjectural: about some there can be no doubt, others are little more than guess-work. The actual traces visible in the manuscript are indicated in the footnotes. All errors that can be emended with reasonable confidence are corrected in the text. When it is only a matter of supplying a letter or a word this is printed within square brackets in the text and no further notice is taken of it, unless to record the author of the emendation in the footnotes. When, however, one reading has had to be substituted for another, the displaced original is recorded at the foot of the page with a reference-number in the text. This does not apply to alterations in the punctuation, which are only recorded, if at all, in the lower range of footnotes. These notes also include difficulties and alterations of reading and other points that call for record. Deletions of any extent or significance are recorded in the notes but are ignored in the text. Suspected errors are dealt with in the glossary.

POSTSCRIPT

I owe the following corrections to Dr. Onions.

Line 3. The manuscript reading 'tentreacte' for 'to entreat' may stand. Though not recorded, the spelling is evidently due to influence of the Latin *tractare*.

Line 1194. 'the gyptian' is a misdivision of 'thegyptian', 'th'Egyptian'.

Line 1543. Brandl's emendation is not needed. For the omission of 'have' see *O.E.D.*, s.v. 'will', $v.^1$, senses 40 ℙ and 42 ℙ.

A merye entrelude entitled Respublica made
in the yeare of oure Lorde .1553. and the first
yeare of the moost pr*o*sperous Reigne of o*u*r
moste gracious Soverainge Quene Marye the
first.

The partes and names
of the plaiers.

> The prologue, a poete.
> Avarice, all*ias* policie the vice of the plaie.
> Insolence, all*ias* *Authoritie*, the chief galaunt.
> Oppression, all*ias* *Reformation* an other gallaunt.
> Adulation, all*ias* *Honestie* the third gallaunt.
> People, representing the poore Commontie.
> Respublica, a wydowe.
> Misericordia,
> *Veritas*,
> Iusticia, } fowre Ladies.
> pax,
> Nemesis, the goddes of redresse *and* correction, *A goddesse*.

The prologue.

First helth and successe wit*h* many agoode newe yeare,
Wissed vnto all this moste noble presence heare.
I have more tentreate[1] youe of gentle Sufferaunce,
That this our matier may have quyet vtteraunce.   4
we that are thactours have o*u*rselves dedicate
with some Christmas devise y*ou*r spirites to recreate
And our poete trusteth the thinge we shall recyte
maye withowte offence the hearers myndes delyte.   8
In dede no man speaketh word*es* so well fore pondred
But the same by some meanes maye be misconstred,[2]
Nor nothinge so well ment, but that by somme p*re*tence
ytt maie be wronge interp*re*ted from the auctors sence.   12
But let this be taken no wurse then yt ys mente

---

[1] MS tentreacte   [2] MS misconstrued,

D.P. Adulation] d *altered.*   10 some] *a final* s *deleted.*

And I hope nor we nor owre poete shalbe shente.
But nowe of thargumente to towch a worde or twayne
the Name of *our* playe ys Respublica certaine 16
oure meaninge ys (I saie not, as by plaine storye,
but as yt were in figure by an allegorye)
To shewe that all Commen weales Ruin *and* decaye
from tyme to tyme hath been, ys, and shalbe alwaie, 20
whan Insolence, Flaterie, Opression, F. 360^b
and Avarice have the Rewle in theire possession.
But thoughe these vices bycloked collusyon
And by counterfaicte Names, hidden theire abusion 24
Do Reigne for a while to comon weales p*r*eiudice
pervertinge all right and all ordre of true Iustice
yet tyme trieth all and tyme bringeth truth to lyght
that wronge maye not ever still reigne in place of right. 28
for whan pleaseth god suche comon weales to restore
To theire welthe *and* honoure wherin thei were afore
he sendeth downe his mooste tendre Compassion
to cause truth goe abowte in visitation. 32
veritee the daughter of sage old Father Tyme
Shewith all as yt ys bee ytt vertue or Cryme.
than dooeth Iustice all suche as Com*m*on Weale oppresse
Tempered with mercye endevoure to suppresse. 36
with whome anone is lynked tranquillitee and peace/
to Common weales Ioye and p*er*petuall encreace.
But shall boyes (saith some nowe) of suche highe mattiers plaie?
No not as disscussers, but yet the booke dothe saie 40
*Ex ore infantiu*m *perfecisti Laudem,*
for whan Criste came rydinge into *Hieresalem,*
The yong babes with tholde folke cryed owte all *and* some,
blessed bee the man that in the Lordes name dothe come. 44
Soo for goode Englande sake this p*re*sente howre *and* daie
In hope of hir restoring from hir late decaye,
we children to youe olde folke, bothe wit*h* harte *and* voyce
maie Ioyne all togither to thanke god *and* Reioyce 48
That he hath sent Marye o*ur* Soveraigne *and* Quene
to reforme thabuses which hithertoo hath been,

31 downe *interlined with caret.* 32 go *deleted after* to *and* g *after* cause   39 plaie?] MS plaie

And that yls whiche long tyme have reigned vncorrecte
shall nowe foreue*r* bee redressed w*i*th effecte.   52
She is oure most wise/ *and* most worthie Nemesis
Of whome o*ur* plaie meneth tamende *that* is amysse.
Whiche to bring to passe *that* she maye have tyme *and* space
Leat vs booth yong *and* olde to godde commend her grace/   56
Nowe yf yowe so please, I wyll goe, *and* hither send,
That shall make youe laughe well yf ye abide thend.

Finis.

Actus primi scena prima.   F. 361ª

Avaryce.

Now godd[i]ggod every chone bothe greate and smale
from highest to lowest Goddiggod to yowe all.   60
Goddiggod what sholde I saie? even or morowe?[1]
if I marke howe the daie goeth god geve me sorowe.
But goddiggod echone twentie and twentie skore
of that ye most lo*n*ge for what wolde ye have more?   64
ye muste p*a*rdoune my wytt*es*/ for I tell youe plaine
I have a hive of humble bees swarmynge in my braine
and he that hath the compace to fetch *that* I must fetche
I maie saie in Counsaile, had nede his wytt*es* to stretche.   68
But nowe what my name is, *and* what is my purpose
Takinge youe all for frend*es* I feare not to disclose.
My veray trewe vnchristen Name ys Avarice
which I may not have openlye knowen in no wise,   72
For though to moste men I am founde Commodius
yet to those that vse me my name is Odius
For who is so foolishe that the evell he hath wrought
for his owen behouff he wolde to light sholde be brought? 76
or who hadnot rather, his ill doing*es* to hide,
Thenne to have the same bruted on everye syde?
Therefore to worke my feate I will my name disguise
And call my Name polycie in stede of Covetise.   80

---

[1] MS morne

55 space *altered from* place (*by prefixing* s *and deleting* l).   61 morowe?]
emend. ed.   64 more?] MS more   70 Takinge] k *altered, perhaps from*
lk   75 evell] *first* e *added.*   76 brought?] MS brought

The Name of policie ys praised of eche one
But to rake grumle sede Avaryce ys a Lone.
The Name of policie is of none suspected,
Polycye is ner of any cryme detected, 84
So that vnder the Name and cloke of policie
Avaryce maie weorke fac*tes and* scape all Ielousie.
And nowe ys the tyme come that except I be a beaste
een to make vp my mouth and to feather my neste 88
A tyme that I have wayted for, a greate Longe space
and nowe maie I spede my purpose If I have grace.
For heare ye sirrha? our greate graund Ladie mother
Noble dame Respublica, she and none other 92
of the offalles, the refuse, the Ragges, the parin*ges*
The baggage, the trashe, the fragmen*tes*, the sharin*ges*
The od end*es*, the Cr[u]mes, the driblet*es*, the chippin*ges*
The patches, the peces, the broklett*es*, the drippin*ges* 96
The fliettance, the scrapin*ges*, the wilde wai[v]es and straies
The skimmyn*ges*, the gubbins of booties and praies
The glenyn*ges*, the casualties, the blynde excheat*es*, F. 361[b]
The forginge of forfayct*es*, the scape of extraict*es*, 100
Thexcesse, the waste, the spoile, the supe*r*fluites,
The windefalles, the shriddin*ges*, the flycyn*ges*/ *th*e petie fees
with à Thowsaunde thin*ges* mo w*hi*ch she maye right well lacke,
woulde fyll all these same purses *that* hange att my bakke/ 104
yea and tenne tymes as manye moo bagges as these
w*hi*ch sholde be but a flea bytinge for hir to lese
That if I maie have the grace, *and* happe, to blynde her
I doubte not a shewete Ladye I shall fy*n*de hir. 108
to hir ytt wer nothing yet manye a smale makith a greate
And all thinge wolde helpe me what ever I maye geate.
full lytle knowe men the greate nede *that* I am yn,
doo not I spende dailie of that that I doo wynne? 112
then age cometh on and what ys a lytle golde
to kepe a man by drede *that* is feble a⟨n⟩d olde?
no man therefore blame me/ thoughe I wolde have more/

95 Crumes] *emend. Brandl, Magnus.*   97 waives] *emend. Magnus*
(waiues).   112 wynne?] MS wynne.   114 by drede] *Magnus conj.*
by brede (by bread): *but?* by = from.   olde?] MS olde

the worlde waxeth harde *and* store (thei saie) is no sore. 116
Nowe the chaunce of theves, in goode houre be ytt spoken—
owte alas I feare I lefte my Cofer Open.
I am surelye vndoone/ alas where be my Cayes?
It ys gone *that* I have swette for/ all my lyve daies. 120
wo worthe all whoreson theves/ *and* suche covetous knaves
that for theire wyndinge sheete/ wolde scrape men owt of theire
 graves. *Exeat.*

Actus primi scena secunda.

*Adulacion, Insolence, Oppressyon/ Intra*nt *canta*[*n*]*tes.*

Adulacion. Oh noble Insolence if I coulde singe as well
 I wolde looke in heaven emonge Angells to dwell. 124
I[*n*]*solence.* Sing? howe doo I sing, but as other manye doe?
Adulacion. yes, an Angels voice ye have to herken vnto.
Insolence. yea, but what availeth that to highe dignitiee?
Oppression. By his armes not a whitte, as farre as I can see. 128
Inso. Or what helpeth that thinge, to sett a man a lofte?
Oppression. By his woundes not a strawe/ so have I tolde yowe
 ofte. F. 362ᵃ
Adul. No but ye are one of suche goodlye p*er*sonage
 of suche wytte *and* beawtye and of sage parentage 132
 So excelente in all poynt*es* of everye arte—
Inso. In dede god and nature in me have done their p*ar*te.
Adul. That yf ye will putte yo*ur*selfe forwarde to the mooste,
 ye maie throughowte the whole lande rewle all the Roste. 136
 howe saie yowe oppression? ys ytt not even so?
Oppr. Thowe saiest soothe Adulacion so mowte I goe.
 if he wer disposed to take the charge in hande,
 I warraunte hym a chive to Rewle all the whole lande. 140
Adul. Lo maister Insolence ye heare Oppression?
Inso. I thanke boothe hime and thee goode Adulacion,
 And Long have I dreamed of suche an enterpryse
 But howe or where to be gynne I cannot devise. 144

117 spoken—] MS spoken. 119 Cayes?] MS Cayes 123 head.
cantantes] *emend. Brandl, Magnus.* 133 arte—] MS arte. 136
lande *interlined with caret.*

*Op*pression. Wherefore serve frend*es*, but y*our* enterpryse to allowe?
Adul. And than must youe supporte them, as thei muste maintayne youe.
Opp. And wherefore do frend*es* serve, but to sett youe yn?
Adul. ye shall have all my healpe/ whan ever ye beginne.   148
Inso. But we maie herein, nothing attempte in no wyse w*i*thowte the Counsaile of *our* fownder Avaryce.
Adul. He muste directe all this geare by his holye gooste.
Oppr. For he knowith whatt ys to be done in eche cooste   152
he knoweth where *and* howe that money is to be hadde
And yond*er* he cometh me thinketh more then half madde.
Intrat Avar.

Actus primi scena tertia.

Avarice. Insolence. Oppression. Adulacion.

Avarice. It was a faire grace *that* I was not vndooen clene
yet my kye was safe lockt vnd*er* nyne lock*es* I wene   156
but een as against suche a thing my harte wyll throbbe.
I fownde knaves abowte my howse readye me to Robbe.
Theare was suche tooting suche looking *and* suche priinge
suche herkenynge/ suche stalking, suche watching, suche spyinge.
what wolde ye my maisters? we looke after a catte.   F. 362b
what make ye heareabowt? we have smelled a ratte.
Nowe a wheale on suche noses thought I by and by,
That so quicklye canne sente where hidden golde dothe lye. 164
But had I not come when I dyd w*i*thowte all failles
I thinke theye had digged vp my walles w*i*th theire nailes.
Inso. Let vs speake to hym and breake his chafing talke.
Avar. Suche gredinesse of Money emonge men dothe walke,   168
That have yt they wyll eyther by hooke or by crooke—
Oppr. lett vs call to hym *that* he maye this waye Looke.
Avar. whether by right or by wronge, in feith some care not.
Therefore catche that catche maye hardely *and* spare not— 172

145 frendes] *the contraction for* -es *is of an unusual form but is found again in* 205 wordes *and* 469 frendes   148 beginne.] MS beginne?
169 crooke—] MS crooke   172 not—] MS not.

Adul. All Haille oure Fownder *and* chief m*aister* Avaryce.
Avar. the devyll ys a knave an I catche not a flyce—
Adul. when ye see yo*ur* tyme looke this waie yo*ur* frend*es* vppon.
Avar. I doubte not to skamble and rake as well as one— 176
Adul. heare bee that wolde faine bee desiples of yo*ur* arte.
Avar. I wilnot bee behinde to gette a childes p*ar*te.
Adul. Nowe if ye have done/ I p*r*ay youe looke this waye
   backe. 179
Avar. Whoo buzzeth in myne eare so? what? ye sawecye Iacke?
Adul. Are ye yet at leysure w*i*th yo*ur* good frendes to talke?
Avar. what clawest thowe myne elbowe pratlinge m*er*chaunt?
   walke.
   ye flaterabundus yowe, youe flyering clawbacke youe 183
   youe the Crowe is white youe, youe the swanne is blacke youe,
   youe Iohn Holde my stafe youe/ youe what is the clocke youe
   youe *ait aio* youe, yowe *negat nego* yowe.
Adul. I mervaile yowe speake to me in suche facion. 187
Avar. whi troublest thowe me then in my contemplacion?
Adul. I came of right goode love not myndinge youe to lett.
Avar. Thowe ner camst to anie man of good love yett. 190
Adul. And these mennes mynd*es* yt was I sholde soo dooe.
Avar. As false wretches as thyne owen selfe and falser tooe. F.363ᵃ
Ins. et oppr. we have been loving to yowe *and* faithfull alwaye.
Avarice. For yo*ur* owne p*ro*fitt*es* thenne *and* not myne I dare saie
   And een verai youe three it was *and* others none
   that wolde have Robbed me not yet haulf an howre gone. 196
Insol. Oppr. Adula. we never robbed anye manne later or rather.
Avar. Yes manye a tyme *and* ofte your owne veraie Father.
Oppr. And to yowe have we borne hartie favors alwaie.
Avar. And I warraunte youe Hangd for yo*ur* labours one daie. 200
Oppr. Adul. Even as oure god we have alwaie Honered youe.
Avar. And een as y*our* god I have aie succoured youe.
Oppr. Wee call yowe o*ur* fownd*er* by all holye Halowes.
Avar. Founder me no foundring, but beware the galowes. 204
Inso. I praie youe leave thes word*es*/ *and* talke frendlie at laste.
Avar. Content at y*our* request/ my fume is nowe well paste

174 flyce—] MS flyce. 176 one—] MS one. 194-6 These three lines are written in a space left for two only. 197 *Adula* written over *Avar*

And in faith what saithe o*ur* frende Adulacion?
Adul. I wonder at yo*ur* Roughe Communycacion, 208
that ye wolde to me vse word*es* of suche vehemence.
Avar. Feyth manne I spake but even to p*ro*ve yo*ur* pacyence,
that yf thowe haddest grunted or stormed thereat—
Adul. Naie fewe times doe I vse suche lewde manier as that. 212
Avar. Come, shake hand*es and* for euer we twoo bee at one.
Adul. As for grutche in me there shall never remaine none.
Avar. Nowe m*aister* Insolence to yo*ur* ghostelye purpose.
Insol. we accordyd a matier to youe to disclosse. 216
Avar. I vnd*er*stande all youre agreemente *and* accorde
for I laie in yo*ur* bosoms when ye spake the worde,
And I like well the advise of oppression,
And eke of Flatterie for y*our* progression. 220
Inso. If there were matier whereon to worke I care not.
Avar. ye shall have matier enoughe, bee doinge, spare not.
Inso. what? to come to hono*ur* and welthe for vs all three? F.363ᵇ
Avar. Ah than ye coulde be well content to leave owte me. 224
Inso. no for I knowe ye can for yo*ur*selfe well p*ro*vyde.
Avar. Yea that I can *and* for Twentye hundreth besyde.
Adul. Oh wolde Christe goode fownd*er* ye wolde *that* thing open.
Avar. Bones knave wilt thowe have ytt / ere yt can be spoken? 228
Oppr. for the passion of god tell ytt vs with all spede.
Avar. By the crosse not aworde / here is haste made in dede.
Insole. yes good Swete Avarice despatch *and* tell att once.
Avar. Naie then cutte my throte, ye are felowes for the nonce. 232
will ye have a matier before ytt canbe tolde?
If ye will have me tell ytt, ye shall y*our* tonges holde.
whiste, scilence, not aworde / mum / leatte yo*ur* clatt*er* sease.
are ye w*ith* Childe to heare / *and* cannot holde yo*ur* pease? 236
So sir, nowe, Respublica the ladie of Estate
ye knowe nowe latelye is left almoost desolate.
hir welthe ys decayed hir Comforte cleane a goe
and she att hir witt*es* endes what for to saie or doe. 240
fayne wolde she have succoure *and* easemente of hir griefe

---

207 Adulacion?] MS Adulacion.   208–9 These two lines are written in a space left for one only.   211 thereat—] MS thereat.   212 times *interlined with caret before* thinges *deleted.*   223 come] c *blotted.*   228 spoken?] MS spoken.

And highlye advaunce them *that* wolde promise reliefe
suche as wolde warraunte hir spirit*es* to revive
mowght mounte to highe eastate / *and* be most sure to thrive. 244
Inso. So. *Adula.* well saide. *Opp.* hah. *Avar.* what is this hum,
  hah? hum?
Insol. onn forth. *Adul.* goe too. *Op.* tell on. *Avar.* bodye of me.
  Adul. mum.
Avarice. what saie ye? *Inso.* hake. *Adul.* tuff. *Op.* hem. *Av.* who
  haken tuffa hum.
What saie ye? *Oppr.* nothing. *Inso.* not aworde. *Ava.* nor youe
  neither? *Ad.* mum. 248
Avar. dyd ye speake or not? *Ins.* no. *Opp.* no. *Adul.* no. *Ava.* nor
  yet doo not?[1]
Inso. no. *Opp.* no. *Adul.* no. *Op.* no. *Inso.* no. *Adul.* no. *Avar.* that
  that that that that that?
S*ir* I entend dame Respublica tassa[i]lle
and so to crepe in to bee of hir Counsaille. 252
I hope well to bring hir in suche a paradise
that hir selfe shall sue me to have my s*er*vice
Than shall I have tyme *and* poure to bringe in youe three. F.364[a]
Oppression. do this owte of hande found*er, and* first speake for
  me 256
bring me in credyte that my hande be in the pye,
An I gett not elbowe rowme emong them let me lye.
Avar. Naie see an Oppression this eager elfe,
bee not sens more covetous then covetous selfe. 260
Softe be not so hastie I praie youe Sir softe awhile
youe will over the Hedge ere ye come att the stile.
Oppr. I wolde fayne be shouldering *and* r*u*mbeling emonge them.
Avar. Naie I will helpe Iavels as shall wrong them. 264
Adul. I praie youe goode foundre let not me be the laste.
Avar. Thowe shalte be well placed where to thrive verai faste.

---

[1] MS net?

243 reli *deleted before* revive.   248 neither?] MS neither. After this is a deleted line: *Ava.* did ye speake or not? *Ins.* not aworde. *Avar.* nor you neither   249 or not?] MS or not.   250 that . . . that.] MS h*a*s y^t . . . y^t *and Magnus suggests that here* y^t *may stand for* tut (*as a rule in the contruction for that the superior* t *is conventionalized*).   251 tassaille] *emend. Magnus.*   255 Before this line is a speech-rule but no speaker's name.   258 *Two letters (perhaps* th) *are deleted after* them

Adul. I thanke youe maister Avarice with all my harte.
Avar. And when thoue arte in place see thowe plaie well thie
　parte 268
　Whan ye clawe hir elbowe remembre your best frende,
　and lett my Commendacions be ever att one ende.
Adul. I warraunte youe. *Insol.* And what shall [I] bee left cleane
　owte?
Avar. No syr, ye shall bee chiefe to bring all things abowte. 272
　ye shall emonges vs have the chiefe preeminence,
　And we to youe as yt were, oughe obedience.
　ye shalbe our leader, our Captaine, and our guyde
　Than must ye looke a lofte with thandes vnder the side. 276
　I shall tell Respublica ye can beste governe,
　bee not ye than skeymishe to take in hand the stern
　than shall we assiste youe as frendes of perfitte truste,
　to doe and to vndoe and Commaunde what ye luste 280
　And when youe have all att your owne will and pleasure
　parte of your lyvinges to your frendes ye maie measure
　and punishe the prowdeste of theim that will resiste.
Oppr. He that ones wincheth shall fele the waite of my fiste. 284
Adul. yea we muste all holde and cleve togither like burres.
Avar. yea see ye three hang and drawe togither like furres.
Oppr. And so shall we be sure, to gett store of money,
　Sweter then sugar. *Avar.* sweter then enie honey. 288
Insol. verai well spoken, this geare will right well accorde. F. 364ᵇ
Adul. didnot I saie ye were worthie to be a lorde?
Avar. I will make Insolence a lorde of highe eastate.
Insol. And I will take vppon me well bothe earelye and late. 292
Oppr. But Insolence when ye come to the encrochinge of landes
　ye maie not take all alone into youre handes
　I will looke to have parte of goodes landes and plate.
Insole. Ye shall have enoughe eche bodye after his rate. 296
Adul. I muste have parte too/ ye muste not have all alone.
Inso. Thowe shalte bee laden tyll thye shoulders shall cracke and
　grone.

　　267 thanke] a *altered from* i　　　271 shall I] *emend. Brandl approved
by Magnus.*　　　277 g *deleted before* can　　　278 stern] n *altered from* l
286 furres] *i.e. thieves.* In the margin is the gloss *of fur furis* (the first *u* is
blotted): it is certainly in the hand of the scribe, the final *s* is unmistakable (cf. e.g. *currentes* at 949).

Adul. I praie youe lett me have a goode Lordship or twoo.
Insol. Respublica shall feede the/tyll thowe wilt⟨te⟩ saie hoo. 300
Adul. And I muste have goode mannour places twoo or three.
Insole. But the chiefe and beste Lordship muste remaine to me.
Oppr. masse/ and I will looke to be served of the beste,
orels some folke some where shall sytt but in smale reste. 304
Insol. I muste have castels *and* Townes in everye shiere.
Adul. And I chaunge of howses one heare/ *and* another there.
Inso. And I muste have pastures/ *and* townships *and* woodes.
Oppr. And I muste nedes have store of golde *and* other goodes. 308
Insolence. And I must have chaunge of Farmes *and* pastures for shepe,
with dailie revenues my lustye porte for to kepe.
Avar. I wolde have a bone here rather then a grote
to make thes Snarling curres gnawe owte eche others throte. 312
here be eager whelpes loe: to yt Boye/ box him balle.
poore I, maie picke strawes/ these hungri dogges will snatche all.
Oppr. Eche man snatche for hym selfe by gosse I wilbe spedde.
Avar. Lacke who lacke shall/ Oppression wilbe corne fedde.
Is not dame Respublica sure of goode handlinge 317
whan theis whelpes, ere they have ytt/ fall thus to skambling?
And me their chiefe Fownder/ thei have een syns forgotte.
Insolence. Thowe shalte have golde *and* silver enoughe to thy
lotte, F. 365ᵃ
Respublica hath enoughe to fill all oure lappes.
Adul. Than I praie youe sir leate oure fownder have some scrappes.
Avar. Scr[a]ppes ye doultishe lowte? fede youe your founder with scrappes?
yf youe were well served/ youre head wolde have some rappes.
Adul. I spake of goode will. *Inso.* Naie fight not good Avarice. 325
Oppr. What enie of vs getteth/ thoue haste the chiefe price.
Avar. Than what ever ye doe ye will remembre me?
Insol. Oppr. Adul. yea. *Avar.* well so doe than, *and* I forgeve youe all three.

<small>300 the] *i.e.* thee *as often (Magnus habitually supplies the second e in brackets, sometimes incorrectly).* 301 mannour] *another superior letter (probably s) is deleted after the* r 323 Scrappes] *emend. Magnus.* your] *the scribe first wrote an ordinary superior* r *and then substituted the conventionalized form.* scrappes?] MS scrappes</small>

Insol. But when doe wee enter everye man his Charge? 329
Avar. as soone as I can spye Respublica att large
  I will bourde hir, and I trowe so wynne hir favoure
  that she sh⟨a⟩ll hire me/ and paie well for my laboure. 332
  than wyll I comende the vertues of youe three
  that she shall praie *and* wishe vnd*er* our Rewle to bee.
  Therefore from this houre bee ye all in readinesse.
Oppr. Doubte not of vs thowe seeste all oure gredinesse. 336
Insol. If ytt bee at midnight, I come att the firste call.
                    they go foorthwarde one after other.
Adul. Doe but whistle for me, and I come foorth with all.
Avar. That is well spoken. I love suche atowarde twygg.
(*he whistleth. Adul.* I come fownd*er*. *Avar. that* is myne owne
  good spaig[n]ell Rigg. 340
  And come on backe againe all three, come bakke agayne.
Insol. Owre found*er* calleth vs backe. *Oppr.* retourne then
  amaigne.

Actus Primi scena quarta.

Avaryce. Adulacion. Insolence. Oppression.

Avar. Come on syrs all three. And first to youe best be truste
  What is y*our* brainpan stufte w*i*th all? wull or sawe duste? 344
Adul. why so? *Avar.* what is y*our* name? *Adul.* Flatterie.
  Avar. een so iust?
Adul. Yea, orels Adulacion if youe so luste,
  Either name is well knowne to mannye a bodye.
Avar. An honest mome, ah ye dolt, ye lowte, ye nodye. 348
  shall Respublica here youre commendac*i*on,
  by the name of Flatterie or Adulacion?
  or when ye Commende me to hir, will ye saie this
  Forsouthe his name is Avarice or Covetise? 352
  And youe that sholde have wytte/ yst y*our* descretion F. 365ᵇ
  Bluntlye to goe forth, and be called Oppression?

329 when *interlined with caret.* Charge?] MS Charge. 343 There seems no reason for a new scene since the characters are the same as before: apparently Adulation, Insolence, and Oppression go out and are immediately recalled by Avarice. 344 wull] u *altered from* l duste?] MS duste 345 name?] MS name. 350 Adulacion?] MS Adulacion. 353 *Insol.* deleted before this line. 354 Oppression?] MS Oppression.

and youe Insolence doe ye thinke yt wolde well frame
  If ye were presented to hir vnder that name? 356
Insol. I thought nothing therevppon by my holydome.
Oppre. My mynde was an other waie by my christendome.
Adul. that thing was lest parte of my thowght by Saincte denie.
Avar. No Marie your myndes were all on your haulfe penie. 360
  but my maisters I must on myne honestie passe,
  And not Ronne on heade, like a brute beaste or an asse
  For is not Oppression eche where sore hated?
  and is not flaterie openly rahated? 364
  And am not I Avarice styll cryed owte vppon?
Adul. Yes I coulde have tolde youe *that*, agreate ⟨w⟩hile agone
  but I woulde not displease youe. *Avar.* and youe Insolence
  I have harde youe ill spoken of a greate waie hens. 368
Adul. In my consciens the devill hym selfe dothe love youe.
Avar. But chaungeyng your yll name fewer shall reprove youe
  as I myne owen self where my name is knowen
  Am right sore assailed to be over throwen 372
  But dooing as I wyll nowe countrefaicte my name
  I spede all my purposes/ *and* yet escape blame.
Inso. Lett vs then have newe names eche manne withowte delaye.
Avar. Els will some of youe make, good hanging stuff one daie 376
Oppr. Thowe must newe christen vs. *Insol.* first what shall my
  name bee?
Avar. Faithe sir your name shalbe mounsyre Authoritie.
Oppr. And for me what ys your determinacyon?
Avar. Marye syr ye shalbe, called Reformacyon. 380
Adul. Nowe I praie yowe devise for me an honest name.
Avar. Thowe arte suche a beaste, I cannot for veray shame.
Adul. If ye thinke good lett me be called Policie.
Avar. Policie. a rope ye shall. Naye *Hipocrisie*. 384
Adul. Fy that were as slaunderous a name a[s] Flatterye.
Avarice. And I kepe for myselfe the name of Policie.
  But if I devise for thee, wilte thowe not shame me? 387
Adul. Naie, I will make the prowde of me, orels blame me. F.366ᵃ

366 while] w *only partly visible.* 369 selfe *interlined with caret.*
377 first *partly enclosed within rules, as if a direction (perhaps they should have enclosed the speaker's prefix).* 379 determinacyon?] MS determinacyon.

Avar. Well than for this tyme thy name shalbe *Honestie.*
Adul. I thanke youe Avaryce. *Honestie, Honestie.*
Avar. Avaryce ye whooresone? Policye I tell the.
Adul. I thanke youe Polycye. Honestie, Honestie. 392
　Howe saie youe Insolence? I am nowe *Honestie.*
Avar. We shall att length have a knave of youe *Honestie.*
　Sayde not I he sholde be called mounsier Authoritye?
Adulacion. Oh frende Oppression, *Honestie, Honestie.* 396
Avar. Oppression? hah? is the devyll in thye brayne?
　Take hede, or in faithe ye are flatterye againe.
　Policie, Reformacion, *Authoritie.*
Adul. Hipocrysie, Diffamacion, *Authorytie.* 400
Avar. Hipocrisye, hah? Hipocrisie, ye dull asse?
Adul. Thowe namedste Hipocrisie even nowe by the masse.
Avaryce. Polycye I saide, policye knave polycye.
　Nowe saye as I sayd. *Adul.* Policie knave policie / 404
Avar. And what callest thowe hym here? *Adul.* Dyffamacion.
Avar. I tolde the he shoulde be called Reformacion.
Adul. veraye well. *Avar.* What ys he nowe? *Adul.* Deforma-
　cion.
Avarice. Was ever the like asse borne in all nacions? 408
Adul. A pestell on hym, he comes of the Acyons.
Avar. Come on, ye shall Learne to solfe: Reformacion.
　Sing on nowe. Re. *Adul.* Re. *Avar.* Refor. *Adul.* Reforma-
　cion.
Avar. Policie, Reformacion, Authorytie. 412
Adulacion. Polycie, Reformacion and Honestie.
Avar. In faithe ye asse yf yo*ur* tong make enie moo trips
　ye shall bothe be flatterie and have on the lips.
　And now mounsyre Authoritie agai*n*st I youe call 416
　ye muste have other garment*es*, and soo muste ye all
　ye muste for the season, counterfaite gravitee.
Ins. et oppr. yes, what els? *Adul.* And I muste counte*r*faite
　honestie.
Avar. And I must tourne my gowne in *and* owte I wene 420
　for theise gaping purses maie in no wyse be seen.

395 Authoritye?] MS Authoritye 403 *Avaryce* written over *policie*
407 After this a line is left blank, and a rhyme seems to be missing. 409
Acyons] A *appears to be written over some small letter.*

I will tourne ytt een here. come helpe me honestye.
Adul. here at hande. *Avar.* why, how now? plaie the knave
    honestie?
helpe, what dooest thowe nowe? *Adul.* I count*er*faicte
    honestie.   424
Avar. Why than come thowe; helpe me, my frende Oppression.
    what helpe calle youe that? *Oppr.* fytt for yo*ur* discrecion.
Avar. Oh I shoulde have sayde, helpe sir Reformacyon.
Oppr. Yea Marye sir that is my nomynacion.   428
Avar. And whan yowe are [in] yo*ur* Robe, keape yt afore close.
Oppr. I praie youe maister policie for what purpose?
Avar. All folke wyll take youe if theye piepe vnd*er* yo*ur* gowne
    for the veriest catif in Countrey or towne.   432
    Now goe, *and* when I call, see that ye readie be.
Inso. I will. *Oppr.* And I wyll. *Adul.* And so will I honestie.
        exeant.
Avar. Well nowe will I departe hens also for a space
    And to bourde Respublica waite a tyme of grace.   436
    ⟨w⟩herever I fynde hir a tyme convenie⟨n⟩t
    I shall saie and dooe that maie bee expedient.
        exeat Avar.

Actus secundi scena prima.

Respublica.

Respublica. Lorde what yearethlye thinge is p*er*manent or stable,
    or what is all this worlde but a lumpe mutable?   440
    who woulde have thowght that I from so florent estate
    coulde have been browght so base as I am made of Late?
    But as the waving seas, doe flowe *and* ebbe by course,
    So all thing*es* els doe chaunge to better and to wurse.   444
    Greate Cyties *and* their fame in tyme dooe fade and passe
    Nowe is a Champion fielde where noble Troie was.
    where is the greate Empire of the Medes *and* persans?
    where bee tholde conquestes of the puissaunt Grecians?   448

---

429 in] *emend. Brandl, Magnus.*   430 purpose?] MS purpose.   437 wherever] *the w is only partially visible.* convenient] *no trace of the third n remains.*   438 expedient.] MS expedient?   441 MS has a question-mark at the end of this line instead of 442.

where Babilon? where Athennes? where Corinth so wyde?
are thei not consumed with all their pompe *and* pryde?
what is the cause heareof mannes wytte cannot discusse
but of Long contynuaunce the thing is founde thus. 452
yet by all experience thus muche is well seen
That in Comon weales while goode governors have been
All thing hath p*r*ospered, and where suche men dooe lacke
Comon weales decaye, and all thing*es* do goe backe. 456
what m*er*vaile then yf I wanting a perfecte staigh
From mooste flourishing welth bee falen in decaye?
But lyke as by default quicke ruine dothe befalle
So maie good governemente att ons recover all. 460
   *Intrat Avar. cogitabund*us *et ludibund*us.

Actus secundi scena Secunda.   F. 367ᵃ
Avaricia: Respublica.

Avar. Alas my swete bag*es* howe lanke and emptye ye bee?
but in faithe and trawth sirs the fawlte ys not in mee.
Respubl. well my helpe and Comforte oh lorde must come from
 thee.
Avar. And my swete purses heare I praie youe all see see, 464
how the litle foole[s] gaspe *and* gape for grumble sede.
Resp. Iff ytt be thie will lorde send some redresse with spede.
Avar. But in faithe goode swete fooles yt shall cost me a fall,
but I will shortelye fyll youe; *and* stoppe yo*ur* mouthes all. 468
Resp. Oh, that ytt were my happe, on frendelye frend*es* to light—
Avar. Hahe? who is that same; *that* speaketh yond*er* in sight?
Who ist? Respublica? yea by the marye masse.
Respub. Than might I bee againe, aswell as ere I was. 472
Avar. ⟨H⟩ide, vp th⟨es⟩e pipes, nowe I praie god she bee blynde,
I am haulf a fraide leste she have an yei be hynde.
we must nowe chaunge o*ur* Coppie: oh lorde whowe I fraie,
lest she sawe my toyes *and* harde whatt I dyd saie. 476
Respub. Is there no good manne that on me wyll have mercye?

450 pryde?] MS pryde.   455 prospered,] MS prospered?   461 bee?]
MS bee   465 fooles] *emend. Brandl, Magnus.*   469 light—] MS light
473 Hide] H *defective.*   these] s *partly visible.*   477 mercye?] MS
mercye.

II. ii]   RESPUBLICA.   17

Avar. Remembre nowe my name ys maister policie.
  all thing I tell yowe muste nowe goe by policie.
Resp. Herke; me thinke I heare the name of polycye.   480
Avar. Hooe calleth Conscience? heare am I polycie.
Resp. I praie youe come to me if youe bee policie.
Avar. yea forsouth, yea forsouthe, my name ys polycye.
Resp. I am sore decaied throughe defalte of polycye.   484
Avar. yea, moost noble Respublica, I knowe that well,
  And doe more lament yt, then enie tong can tell.
  For an if goode policie had had youe in hande,
  ye had nowe been the wealthiest in anye lande.   488
  but good policie hath long been putte to exile.
Resp. yea god wotte ye have been bard from me agreate while.
Avar. yea, I have been putte backe, as one cleane of shaken,
  And what can a man doe, tyll he be forthe taken?   492
Resp. well I fele the lacke of your helping hande by the Roode.
Avar. Alacke noble ladye I woulde I coulde doo youe goode.
Respub. yes policie ye might amende all if youe luste.   F. 367ᵇ
Avar. yea feithe, I durste put miself to youe of truste   496
  but there bee enoughe that for youe coulde shifte make.
Respublica. yet none like to yowe, if yowe woulde yt vnder take,
  and I will putt miselfe whollye into your handes,
  Metall, graine, cataill, treasure, goodes and landes.   500
Avar. well I will take some paine but this to youe be knowen,
  I will doe ytt, not for your sake, but for myne owne.
Respub. Howe saie ye *that* policie? *Avar.* this to yowe bee knowen,
  I will doe all for your sake, and not for myne owen.   504
Resp. I thanke youe policie. *Avar.* naie I thanke youe ladye
  And I trust ere long to ease all [y]oure maladie.
  will ye putte yourselfe nowe wholye into my handes?

480 me] MS (me   484 decaied] *the first* d *is written over* t   492 taken?] MS taken.   502 owne] *there may be another* e *interlined and the first minim of the* n *appears to have been added.*   505 From here on, where a line is divided between two or more speakers, the first prefix in the line is sometimes followed by a small paragraph resembling a Greek σ.   506 youre] *emend. ed.*   507 will] MS will, (*the rather badly written word being perhaps mistaken for* well: *indeed an attempt may have been made to alter the* i *to* e).

Resp. ordre me as youe wyll. *Avar.* Treasure good*es and*
 land*es*? 508
Resp. yea everye whitte. *Avar.* well, I thanke youe ons againe.
 But nowe that youe maie thinke / my dealing trewe *and* plaine,
 And because one cannot doe so well as ⟨m⟩annye,
 ye¹ muste associate me with mo compaignie 512
 And first by my will ye shall sette vp honestie.
Resp. Marye, w*i*th all my veraie harte: but where is he?
Avar. veray hard to fynde: but I thinke I coulde fett² hym.
Resp. Call him straight waies hither, see that nothing lett hym. 516
Avar. It were best if I shall goe fett men for the nones
 to make but one viage, *and* bring them all att ones.
Resp. whome more then hym? *Avar.* ye muste stablishe
 Authoritie.
Resp. that muste needes bee doen. *Avar.* and eke Reforma-
 cion. 520
 wee fowre will rewle thing*es* of an other facion.
Resp. Polycye I praie youe goe fette all these straight waye.
Avar. yes, for this yo*ur pr*esent case maie byde no delaye,
 I will goe *and* come wyth all Festinac*i*on. *exeat.* 524
Resp. I like well this trade of Administrac*i*on
 policie for to devise for my Comoditie
 no p*e*rsonne to be advaunced but honestye,
 then Reformacion good holsome lawes to make 528
 And Auctorytie see the same effecte maie take
 what comon weale shall then bee so happie as I?
 For this (I p*e*rceive) is the drifte of policie.
  Intrat Avarice ad ducens Insol. oppr. et adulac.
 And beholde where he is retourned againe seens, 532
 Hee shewith himselfe aman of muche diligence.

---

¹ MS yea   ² MS fetche

511 mannye] m *defective.*   512 ye] *emend. Magnus.*   515 fett] *emend. Magnus.*   519 A riming line appears to be missing.   520 *Avar.* interlined with caret.   527 honestye,] MS honestye?   529 make *deleted before* take   531 policie.] MS policie?

Actus secundi scena tertia. F. 368ᵃ

Adulacion. Avaryce. Respublica. Insolence. Oppression.

Adul. I will doe hir double servis to another.
Avar. ye double knave youe, will ye never be other?
Adula. she shall have triple service of me honestye. 536
Avar. ye quadrible knave will[1] ye ner vse modestie?
 Thowe dronken whoresone, doest thoue not see nor perceive
 where Respublica standes readie vs to receyve?
Respub. what talke have theye yonder emong them selves to-
 gither? 540
Adul. I have spied hir nowe. shall I first to hir thither?
Avar. Softe lett me present yowe. *Resp.* I weene thei bee in
 feare.
 polycye approche, *and* bring my goode frendes nere.
Avar. Come on my deare frendes *and* execute with good wyll,
 suche offyce as eche of youe shall be putt vntyll. 545
 Dame Respublica yt ys that for youe hathe sent.
 Come on Frendes I will youe vnto her greace present.
Inso. Oppr. ⟨To⟩ serve h⟨i⟩r we are preast with harte *and* whole
 entent. 548
Avar. Madame I have brought youe these men for whom I went.
Respub. Policie I thanke youe/ ye have made spiede spede,
 therefore ye be double welcome/ *and* welcome frendes in dede.
Avar. Madame your grace to serve we all are fullye bente. 552
Adul. And Madame ye shall fynde me double diligente.
Resp. That is spoken of a goode harte: but who bee ye?
Adula. Forsouth madame my name ys maister Honestie.
Resp. honestye? well saide. *Avar.* Madame this is honestie. 556
Adula. yea forsouth an please your grace I am honestee.
Avar. Madame he is for youe: on my woorde regarde hym.
Resp. yes *and* with large preferment I will rewarde hym.

---

[1] MS we

---

534 double *interlined with caret.* another.] MS another? 537 will]
emend. Brandl: Magnus *proposes* wi' 546 Respublica] *a letter* (? u)
deleted between b *and* l 547 her *interlined above a word (apparently*
heyace) *deleted.* 548 To] T *partly visible.* hir] i *partly visible.* 558
woorde] r *interlined with caret.*

Adul. I thanke yo*ur* grace. And I will for youe take suche paine 560
that ere I deserve one / ye shall geve me twayne.
Avar. Honestie yo*ur* tong tripth. *Resp.* howe saide ye, take such
paine—?
Adul. That ere ye geve me one I will des*er*ve twaine.
By y*our* lycence madame to take awaie this mote. 564
Avar. Naie honestie will not see a wemme on yo*ur* Cote.
Nowe vnto youe I commende Reformac*i*on.
Resp. Of hym is no small nede nowe in this nacion.
Oppr. well nowe *that* ye bydde me abuses to redresse 568
I doubte not all enormitis so to represse,
As shall redowne to yo*ur* wealth and hono*ur* att length. F. 368ᵇ
Respub. There to shall Authoritee ayde youe w*i*th his strength.
Avar. yea, for Authoritee to governe ys mooste fytte. 572
Insole. yf ye dame Republica doe me so admytte
I doubte not to hamper the prowdeste of them all.
Resp. And emong youe destroye, Avarice— *Adul.* hem. *Insol.*
et oppr. we shall.
Resp. Vanquishe Oppression and Adulacion, 576
For those three have nighe wrought my desolacion.
Avar. hem, sirs, hem there, kepe y*our* gownes close afore I saie
have ye forgotten nowe what I tolde youe one daye?
There is an other too / that wolde bee chaced hens. 580
Respubl. who is that? *Avar.* Lucifers sonne called Insolence.
Resp. ye saie truth and manye naughtie ones moo then he.
Insol. et oppr. If ye dare truste vs— *Insol.* all— *Oppr.* all shall
reformed bee. 583
Resp. I thanke youe / *and* I truste youe for my maintenaunce
Too bee administer for y*our* goode governaunce.
Insol. Than w*i*thowte feare or care ye maie yo*ur*selfe repose.
Oppr. And lett vs alone withall suche mattiers as¹ those.
Resp. Than I leave yowe heare on our affaires to consoulte. 588
exeat Resp.

---
¹ MS &

560 paine] *apparently* paines *with* s *or* es *erased.* MS has a question-mark
at the end of this line instead of 562.   562 paine—?] MS paine   567
nede *interlined with caret.*   575 Avarice—] MS Avarice.   583 vs—]
MS vs.   all—] MS all.   bee] b *written over another letter, perhaps* w
585 administer] *Magnus emend.* administerd (*wrongly*).   587 as]
emend. Magnus.

Insol. whan youe please in god*es* name.   *Oppr.* we muste bothe
   sifte *and* boulte.
Adul. She is gonne.   *Avar.* well then sirs lett vs make no delaye
   But abowte our markett departe eche manne his waye.
Adul. Naie first lett vs sing a song to lighten our hart*es*.   592
Avar. Than are ye like for me / to sing but of three p*artes*.
   Canne Avarice harte bee sett on a merie pynne
   And see no gaine no profitte att all coming in?
Insol. We shall have enoughe to drive awaie all sorowe.   596
Avar. Than sing wee on bowne viage, and Saincte George the
   borowe.
   Cantent, Bring ye to me and *I to ye,* et cetera *et sic exeant.*

Actus tercij[1] *scena prima.*

Respublica.

Respub. The goode hope that my my*sters* have putt me in
   to recover rewine that in me dothe beginne,
   hathe so recomforted my spirit*es and* myne harte   600
   that I feale muche easemente of my greate greefe *and* smarte.
   nowe I doe lesse woond*er* that lost men life to save,
   Ferre from lande dooe laboure againste the roring wave   F. 369ᵃ
   for hope I see, hathe mightie Operacion   604
   Againste the mortall sting of drouping desperacion.
   nowe if I might but heare what policie hathe wrought   606
   or some one good thing *that* my frend*es* to passe had browght
   I woulde putt no doubt*es* but all thing shoulde soone bee well.
   Loe where Cometh honestie: he wyll the truthe tell.

Actus tercij Scena secunda.

Adulacyon.   Respublyca.

Adul. Three Hundred pounde by yeare and agoode mano*ur* place.
   well, yt ys metely well in so shorte tyme and space.   611

---
[1] MS *tercia*

---

597 *et cetera*] MS has & ccę   598 head. *tercij*] emend. ed.   598
mysters] MS *has* myʳˢ. *perhaps a miswriting of* mʳˢ. (*the* y *may be due to
dittography after* my): *see glossary.*   611 space.] MS space? (*possibly
for* space!).

More will come right shortelye this geare dothe gailie walke.
Bones, heare is Respublica, what vse I suche ta[l]ke?
I seeke ladie Respublica. *Resp.* loe I am here
And welcome honestie. what doe my frend*es* mooste deare? 615
Adul. Certes, madame we reste nor daie nor night nor howre
⟨to p⟩ractise and travaile for yo*ur* welth and honoure.
But/ O/ lorde what a prudente man ys policie
what a depe heade he hathe to devise *and* to spie.
Resp. he is fyne in dede. *Adul.* Also Reformacion. 620
howe earenest he is in his Opperacyon.
Resp. I thinke of hym no lesse. *Adul.* nowe than Authoritee
The stowtest in his offyce that ev*er* I dyd see.
I will no farther prayse them madame/ for doubtelesse 624
theye ferre sormounte all praise *that* my tong can expresse.
yee maie blesse the tyme ye mette with suche as thei bee
And I doe my poore p*ar*te/ *Resp.* I doubte not honestee,
And condinge Rewarde shall ye all have for yo*ur* paine. 628
Adul. I have scarce an howse wherin myselfe to mayntayne.
Respub. Honestie, shall not lacke. *Adul.* I doe not crave nor care.
we shall take but scraps *and* refuse, that ye maie spare.
we willnot encroche the peoples Comoditie 632
we shall take onelie that maie come with honestie.
Respub. Christes blessing have ye. but loe yond*er* cometh people.
Adul. I had thought as soone to have mette here paules
steeple. 635

Actus tercij scena tertia.

People. Adulacion. Respublica.

People. whares Rice puddingcake? I praie god she bee in heale.
Adul. who? Rice puddingcake? *peopl.* yea alese dicts comon-
weale.
Adul. I knowe hir not. *peopl.* masse youe liest valeslye in yo*ur*
harte.
She is this waie. che wart afalse harlot youe arte. F. 369ᵇ

---

613 talke] *emend. Magnus.* 617 to practise] *traces of* to p *remain.*
638–9 youe liest . . . youe arte] *Brandl (introd.) takes* youe *to stand for* poue,
but this is hardly possible in view of your harte

Adul. I knowe Respublica. *peopl.* yea marie whare is shee? 640
Adul. She is buisie nowe/ *peopl.* masse ere iche goe chill hir zee,
    for this waie she came. *Respub.* lett my people come to
    mee.
Adulac. god forbydde els. Come on people is this same shee? 643
Peopl. yea malkin ist. *Resp.* People what wolde youe with me
    nowe?
Peopl. Marye mustres madame my ladie, howe doe youe?
Respub. Even so so people. I thanke youe withall my Harte, 646
    And I hope for better. *Peopl.* Than lett poore volke ha zome
    parte
    vor we Ignoram people whom itche doe perzente
    wer ner zo I polde, zo wrong, and zo I torment.
    Lorde Ihese Christe whan he was I pounst *and* I pilate 650
    was ner zo I trounst as we have been of years late.
Adul. how so? who hathe wrought to youe suche extremytee?
peopl. Naie to tell how zo, passeth our captyvytee.
Respub. It passeth anie mans Imaginacion. 654
people. youe zai zouth, yt passeth anie mans madge mason
    vor we þynke ye love vs as well as ere ye dyd.
Respub. My love towardes youe my people cannot be hydde.
people. And we þinke ye woulde faine wee poore volke did well.
Respub. And better then ere ye dyd/ if howe, I coulde tell.
people. And we þinke ye woulde we zelie poore volke sholde
    thrive. 660
Respub. yea doubtles as anye lyke creature alive.
Adul. What nede ye of hir goode will towardes yowe to doubte?
people. peace thoue with zorowe and let me tell my tall owte.
Respub. Saie on my good people/ let me heare all your mynde.
people. Bum vei we ignoram people beeth not zo blinde 665
    but we passeive, ther falleth of corne *and* cattall
    wull, shepe/ woode, leade, tynne, Iron *and* other metall,
    And of all þinges, enoughe vor goode and badde 668
    and as commediens vor vs, as er we hadde.
    and yet the price of everye thing is zo dere

640 shee?] second e *apparently written over some other letter and question-
mark added.* 658 love vs *deleted after* ye   faine wee] *Magnus* we zelie
(*accidentally anticipated from* 660).   661 MS has a question-mark at the
end of this line instead of 662.   670 dere] MS dere?

as thoughe the grounde dyd bring vorth no suche thing no
where.
Respb. In dede I have enoughe if yt be well ordered, 672
but fewe folke the better yf I bee misordered.
People. Nai now youe zai zouth/ een þieke same waie goeth the
hare.
Ill ordring tis, hath made bothe youe and wee threde bare.
Adulacion. what naughtie folkes were thei? can yowe their names
reade? 676
People. yea that Iscan awhole messe of om for a neade. F. 370^a
There is vorste and vormooste Flatteree ill a þee
A slypper suger mowthed howrecop, as can bee
he fliereth on youe/ *and* beareth vs faire in hande 680
And therewhile robbeth bothe youe *and* we of oure lande.
Than cometh the sowre roughe crabbed childe Oppression
he tumbleth whom a lust oute of possession.
Than ys there the thirde, Iscannot membre his name. 684
what call ye þiekesame felowes? god geve them a shame,
that beeth styll clymbing vp a lofte for premydence
And cannot be content with theire state? *Adul.* Insolence?
people. yea þicke same is he, zorylesse. *Resp.* Naie Insolence.
people. well, hele roile all the roste alone cha harde yt zaide 689
orels make the best of them agaste *and* afraide.
And zuche goode men as coulde *and* woulde ordre youe well
he is so copped he nil not suffre¹ to mell. 692
If theye nylnot be rolde then hence oute of favoure
⟨yea⟩ and perhaps corrupte om zore vor their Laboure.
yet he and thother twaine weorke all after the vice
of cha for yet tone name tother is Covetise. 696
þieke hongri howrecop hathe suche a policate wytte,
That he teacheth them to rake and scrape vp eche whytt.
And zo these vowre, (but it shall never come owt for me)

---

¹ MS ssuffre (ss *perhaps for* S *by analogy with* ff *for* F).

676 reade ?] MS reade   684 name.] MS name ?   685 þiekesame] *Brandl conj.* þickesame; *but see* 697 *where Brandl reads* þicke *erroneously*.   693 oute *interlined with caret.*   694 yea] *the tail of* y *is visible.*   697 *Written in the margin to replace* þieke he teacheth them to rake & scrape vpp eche whit. *deleted. Before the deleted line is a small cross, repeated before the marginal addition; and before* 698 *the letter* b., *repeated at the end of the addition.*

volke thinke will never cease to spoile bothe youe *and* we. 700
vor sometime thei face vs/ and call vs peason knaves
And zwareth goddes bones thei will make vs all slaves.
Tharevore chwas besiraunce your ladidome to zee,
and to geve youe warning. *Resp.* heare ye this *Honestye*? 704
people. well and god emend all and abee zo good a clerke—
Resp. heare ye this honestie? *people.* though tynkers sholde
lacke worke.
Resp. I am putte in comforte all shall shortelye emende.
Adul. itt ys in goode waie alreadye/ els godde defende. 708
Respub. loe people hearest thowe this? bee of good cheare.
peop. yea, iche heare his vaire wor*des*: but what beeth we the
neare?
Respub. People vnd*er*stande ye that this ys *Honestee.*
peopl. whare a bee trowe? masse cha zeen zome as zmothe as
hee 712
have be trial bee vound valse flatterers to bee.
Respub. I take this man for no suche: this ys *Honestee.*
people. A gaye smoult smirking howrecop tis zo mot I þee.
Respub. well credite my word*es* people/ this ys honestee.
People. whan Isfinde ytt, chil beleve yt. *Resp.* tys honestie. 717
people. Iscrye hym mercye than. *Resp.* he and *Authorytee,* F.370ᵇ
Ioignyng w*i*th policie *and* Reformacyon
Travaile to restore tholde welth to this nacion 720
people. whoughe than chil warte all within twoo years as plentye,
as twas eny tyme w*i*thin these yeres twyse twentye.
but how maye we knowe, *and* see that this thyng ys trewe?
Adulacion. ye shall pr*o*ve att length by theffecte *that* shall
ensue. 724
peop. Nai and we shall alwaie bee *se*rved but with shales,
than chil beleve een still/ *tha*t vaire woordes beeth but tales.
Adul. The thing alreadie to suche forwardnes ys browght
that muche to y*our* benefytte ys alreadie wrowght. 728
peop. yea? what any goode acte have ye alreadye doone?
Adul. It ys but yong daies yet, thing*es* are but nowe beegone.
the frewte of o*ur* dooing*es* cannot so soone appeare.

705 clerke—] MS clerke.   708 godde] *one* d *added.*   723 this]
s *written over* n *and a following* g *deleted.*   trewe?] MS trewe.

but people ye shall feele ytt within seve⟨n⟩ y⟨eare.⟩ 732
ye knowe it is no smale weorke from so greate decaie—
Respub. People, he saith truthe. *Adul.* to sett all in good staighe
  therefore bee ye quiet, and hope for a goode ende. 735
people. yes chil tarie laisure/ *and* take what god shall send.
Respub. Than people let vs twaine/ departe in quietnesse,
  For this talking here/ maye hinder theire buisinesse. ⎫
peopl. Come on I chil waite avore youe, and bee yo*ur* ⎬ *exeant.*
  manne. ⎭
Adul. And I will to my fealows as faste as I canne. 740
Bee thei gone? fare well theye/ god sende them bothe the pippe.
but in feith people I will have youe on the hyppe.
I wilbe even with youe for yo*ur* brode carping.
Ah, ye peasaunte wretche, on vs fowre to bee harping. 744
And yet muste we o*ur* mattiers handle descretelye,
orels I feare yt will ende not veraye swetelye.
but nowe I wolde Avarice orels Insolence,
or Oppression were heare rather then six pence. 748
And loe where Avarice comth a woulff in the tale,
(as the p*r*overbe saithe) what dothe he after hym hale?

Actus tercij scena quarta.

Avarice.   Adulacion.[1]

Avar. Come on swete bags of golde/ come on w*ith* a good will
I on youe soo tendre; *and* ye soo frowarde styll? 752
Come forewarde I praie youe swete bags; ah, will ye soo?
Come or I muste drawe youe whether ye will or noo.
I knowe yo*ur* desire ye woulde faine bee in my chest.
when the bealie is full the bones woulde bee att reast. F. 371ᵃ
bee contente awhile I will couche youe all vp soone
where ye shalnot bee spied neither of Sonne nor Mone.
what nowe brother honestie? what prye ye this waie?
is there eni thing here that ys yours, can ye saie? 760

---

[1] MS adds *Oppression.* (but he does not appear till the next scene).

732 seven] *only a trace of* n *remains.*   yeare] *recognizable traces of the damaged letters remain.*   733 decaie—] MS decaie   750 hale?] MS hale.   753 soo?] MS soo.

looke of from my baggs, yt ys a pretye matier,
  ye can see no grene cheese/ but your teethe wyll watier/
Adul. In nomine patris, hast thowe gotte all this syens?
Avar. whi, thinkest thowe I have sett ydle sens I went hens?
  Naie I have filled my lytle purses too eche one. 765
Adul. hast thow so in dede? thowe arte a felowe alone.
Avar. with olde Aungelots and Edwardes I thinke I have.
  Come forthe. how saie ye sir? pepe out ye litle knave.
  howe thinke youe by this bunting? is he full or no? 769
  And his felowes all dothe not theire skinne stretche for wo?
  Now theise litell buttons no bygger then twoo nuttes
  have theye not plaied gluttons, *and* filled well theire guttes?
Adul. But looke who cometh yonder puffing and tuffing.
Avar. Come the devill yf hym luste staring and snuffing. 774

Actus tertij scena quinta.

Oppression.   Avarice.   Adulacion.

Oppr. In all my whole life was I never werier.
Avar. Come nere on goddes halfe the mo knaves the merier.
  where have ye lost your breath? in some cofer dyvinge?
Opp. Shouldring emonges them for a peice of a lyvinge. 778
Adulacion. And what are yowe nowe in any goode hope to
    thryve?
Oppr. Feithe if I luste I maie were myters fowre or fyve
  I have so manye haulfe bisshoprikes at the leaste.
Adul. by tharmes of Callis/ than am I a verye beaste. 782
Avar. why what hast thowe gotten to thie share in this space?
Adul. three hundred pound by the yeare and one manior place.
Avar. Ah the passhen of god/ three hundred pownd *and* no more?
Adul. Is not that faire for hym *that* had nothing before? 786
Avar. what, three hundred pound by years? call the honestee?
  Call thee a knave thowe shamest our fraternitee.
  three hundred pounde? if some man had been in thie rome

---

772 guttes?] MS guttes   779 *Adulacion*] *du* written over *var*   783 space *interlined above* place *deleted.*   786 before?] MS before.   787 honestee?] MS honestee   *After this* MS *has a deleted line:* I tolde them Respublica att theire wealthe dyd grutche (*cf.* 799). *The next five lines are crowded into the space left for four.*

A thowsaunde pounde a yeare/ ere this tyme might have come.
three hunderd pounde a yeare? againste our next metinge, 791
geate more/ or I shall geve [thee] a homlye greetinge.
Adul. he here hathe flytched the bisshoprikes alreadie.
Avar. yea, I can him thanke he hathe been somewhatt spedie.
Oppr. But yet have I left many a goode gobbet looce.   F. 371^b
     Chaunge thoue for the reast/ geve a fether for agooce.   796
Adula. Didst thowe with anie one of them make suche exchaunge?
Oppr. yea I almoste leaft them never a ferme nor graunge.[1]
     I tolde them Respublica at their wealth dyd grutche
     and the fyfte pennie thaye had was for them to muche.   800
     So Authoritee *and* I, did with theim soo choppe
     that we lefte the best of them a threde bare bisshop:
     to some we left one howse, to some we left none,
     The beste had but his see place, that he might kepe home.   804
     we enfourmed them/ *and* we defourmed theym,
     we confourmed them, *and* we refourmed theym.
Adul. And what gave ye theim in your permutacions?
Oppr. Bare parsonages of appropriacions,   808
     bowght from Respublica *and* firste emprowed,
     than at the higheste extente to bisshops allowed,
     leate owte to theire handes for fowrescore *and* ny⟨netee⟩n yeare.
Avar. Loe cosyn honestee loe, doo ye heare this geare?   812
     Faith youer masship will thrive att the latter lammas.
Adul. I nowe graunte myselfe to have been a verye asse,
     but all ys not yet gonne/ in cace I have goode lucke.
Oppr. No there is yet enoughe left, for a better plucke   816
     For some of them were aged *and* yet wouldnot dye,
     and some woulde in no wyse to owre desyres applye.
     But we have Roddes in pysse for them everye chone,
     that they shalbe flyced yf we reigne, one by one.   820
Avar. And howe dyd all frame with our mounsire Authorytee?
Oppr. Att length he wonne the full superiorytee.
Adul. But the rude grosse people at hym repyneth sore,
     and againste vs all fowre with a wyde throte dothe he rore.   824

---

[1] MS graunce

792 thee] *conj. Brandl.*   796 *The first* for *interlined with caret.*   804 his *interlined with caret.*   811 nyneteen] *some traces of the damaged letters remain.*   821 Authorytee?] MS Authorytee.

But softe, peace, me thinketh I here hym hem and hake.[1]
If we mete here all fowre we shall some ordre take.

Actus tercij scena sexta.
Insolence. Adulacion. Oppression. Avarice.

Insolence. what, myne olde frend*es* all three? by my truthe sirs well founde.
Adul. et oppr. feith syr, mooste hartelye welcome into this grownde. 828
Insol. Bones, what have we here? *Avar.* a hah. *Insol.* bags of money, I trowe?
Avar. Have we? naie I have, but none for youe *that* I knowe.
loe sir, thus might an honeste man come to his harmes. F. 372[a]
I will lye downe on them / *and* kepe theym in myne armes. 832
Insol. Haste thowe gotte all this? I miselfe have not so muche.
Avar. Than have ye whole townes *and* castells: I have none suche
yet wyll ye not denie I iudge in my fansie,
that ye gotte theym by the drifte of me Policie. 836
Insol. I confesse that. *Oppr.* all my land*es* are scarce so muche woorth.
Avar. Thei were lesse when I policie firste sett yowe foorth.
Adul. he hathe purses with golde, woulde I had so manie.
Avar. It were pittie *that* suche a gooce shoulde have enie. 840
youre good masship appoincted me to crumes *and* scraps
but Policie wyll lyve by his neighbours perhaps.
But thus I see youe woulde polle me an ye wiste howe
therefore I will goe hoorde yt, I make god a vowe 844
I will make yt sure vnder nyne doores and nyne lockes
⟨And⟩ who but looketh that waie, shall syt in niene stockes.
Insolence. Naie, fyrste declare to vs howe thowe didst all this geate.
Avar. For yo*ur* learning I will youe a spectacle sette 848
but fyrst gette ye from me, *and* stande a goode waie hence,
This shallnot lye within y*our* reache by youre lycence.

---

[1] MS andohake

825 peace,] MS peace? (*perhaps for* peace!). 829 bags] s *written over* ℮ 830 knowe.] MS knowe? 846 And] *traces remain*.

Naie yet farther lest ye take my baggs for bluddinges
for suche hongrye doggs will slabbe vp sluttishe puddinges. 852
Adul. Is yt well nowe? *Avar.* yea, nowe hardelie stand there styll,
And the Names of my baggs to youe declare I will.
Firste and foremoste this bagg is my veraie cleare gaine
of leasses encroched and foorthwith solde againe 856
This bag is myne intresse, of thys yeares vserie
And this is of mattiers bolstred vpp with periurie
This is bribes above my stipende in offecis
This fifth I have by selling of benefices 860
This ys my rentes that my clerkes yearelye render me
to bee *and* contynue in offyce vnder me.
This same I got by sectourshipp of my Mother,
A vengeaunce on hir old witche for suche an other. 864
This bag have I kepte of other sectourships whole,
whiche the madde knaves woulde have[1] scattred by penie dole.
This is of Churche goodes scraped vpp withoute alawe,
For which was as quicke scambling as ever I sawe, 868
of their plate, their iewels, *and* copes, we made them lowtes,
Stopping peoples barking with lynnen rags *and* clowtes,
Thei had thalter clothes thalbes and amices
with the sindons in which wer wrapte the chalices. 872
This nyneth hath beguiled the king of his custome,
This tenth of selling counterfaicte wares hath come. F. 372[b]
Now this eleventh is of tallowe, Butter, Cheese,
Corne, Raweclothes, leather by stelth sent beyonde seaes 876
This twelfth is of grayne, bell meatall, tynne and lead,
Conveighd owte by crekes whan Respublica was in bed
This thirteenth I filled throughe facing owte of dawes
bothe from landes and goodes by pretence of the lawes. 880
Thus these thirteen smale Iobbes are myne by policie
All men must shifte for a poore Lyving honestlye.
If er I bestowe them, yt shalbee the nexte lent
to the prioure of prickingham and his covent. 884
Adul. well nowe we maie come nere maie we not if we lust?

---

[1] MS had

866 have] *emend. ed.*

Avar. ye are nere enoughe: oute of my reache I dare youe trust.
Adul. well, nowe lett vs sing yf ytt please Authoritee
to refreshe oure spirit*es* yt ys restorytee. 888
Insol. I recke not for Compaignie sake to sing once ⟨more.⟩
Avar. I have lesse minde to sing nowe then I had before.
than had I no luste to sing because I was bare,
And nowe howe to kepe that I have gotte I doe care. 892
Oppr. Solace we muste nedes have whan *that* we are werie.
Adul. It *pro*longeth the life of manne to bee merye.
Avar. An if ye sing so muche honestie w*i*thowte faile
Thriste *and* youe at length I feare will make a battaile 896
But goe too, sing on, yf there be no remedie.
An ye looke at my bags ye marre my melodie.
Cantent, Hey noney nony houghe for money et cetera.
Oppr. Now, abought *pro*fitte devide we o*ur*selves abrode.
Avar. yea, and heare ye maisters? while tyme is, laie on lode 900
Consider ye have but a tyme of hey making,
And harvest is not mued w*i*thowte peines taking.
Nowe, tyme willnot tarye *and* therefore take good hede
despache while tyme s*er*veth and all yo*ur* matie[r]s spede. 904
Tyme hath no reine nor bridle / but renneth a pace.
Insol. Marke policies woord*es* / sirs, excellent in our cace.
Avar. And tyme hathe this one vngracious *pro*pertee,
to blab at length *and* open all that he doothe see. 908
Than a daughter eke he hath called veritee,
As vnhappie a longtounged girle as can bee.
she bringeth all to light, some she bring[eth] to shame, F. 373[a]
she careth not a grote what manne hathe thanke or blame.
yf men be praise worthie she dothe so declare them
And if otherwyse in faithe she dothe not spare them.
Oppress. we will feather oure nest*es* ere tyme maye vs espie
or veritee have powre our doing*es* to descrye. 916
Avar. Remembre this verse, *Vt sint omnia salva,*
Fronte capillata, post hec occasio calva.

---

889 more.] *a trace of e alone remains.* 897 goe] *o written over e*
898 S.D. *et cetera.*] MS has *& cc'*. 904 matiers] *emend. Brandl, Magnus.*
909 he] *h altered from y.* 911 bringeth] *emend. Brandl, Magnus (but*
bring *may possibly have been erroneously attracted into concord with the plural*
some).

oppr. Make me vnderstande that fyne rag of rhetorike.
Avar. Loe here a fyne felowe to have a bisshopricke 920
    a verse of latynne he cannot vnderstande,
    yet dareth he presume boldelye to take in hande,
    Into a deanerie or Archdeaconrye to choppe,
    And to have the liveloode awaie from a bisshopp. 924
oppr. ⟨To me shewe⟩ thie verse and leave thys p*er*swasion.
Avar. Forsouthe sir yt was of the goddesse occasyon.
    She weareth a greate long tuffet of heare beefore
    and behinde hathe not one heare/ neither lesse nor more 928
    whereby is taught youe that when Occasyon ys
    ye muste take yt be tyme/ or of yo*ur* purpose mysse.
Adul. Than while Occasion doeth nowe serve soo well,
    I praie youe geve eare to one thing *that* I must tell. 932
Inso. et oppr. what ys that? *Adul.* Mounsire yf ye heare people mumbling
    ye muste storme, *and* sharpelye take hym vp for stumbling.
    ye woulde not thinke what he said alitle while sens
    of vs, to Respublica/ in myne owne presence. 936
Inso. whan I mete theym nexte/ I shall tell them bothe my mynde.
Avar. And policie to helpe youe/ wyll not be behinde.
Adul. Ientle Respublica was soone pacified,
    But people was sturdie *and* woulde not be qualified. 940
Avar. Alas good poore selie sowle beare heare faire in hand
    And ye maie wynne hyr/ as youe lust to vse hyr land.
Oppr. But of goddesse occasion one lytle more.
Avar. Marye sir/ even as I woulde have said before, 944
    she standeth with winged feete on a rolling whele
    to take flyght or anie grasse, maie growe on hir hele,
    And even while we stand Iangling in this presence,
    I dare saie she is flowen twise twentie score myle hence. 948
Oppr. yea? cock*es* bones/ than Adew. *Insol.* farewell/ *Adul.*
    and I am gone.   *exeant currentes.*
Avar. Feithe and have after, as faste as I can, anon.   F. 373[b]

925 To me shewe] *traces of* s *and* h *and possible traces of* T *and the final* e *remain. Brandl suggested* Beschrewe *and* Magnus A mercie, shewe *but the first letter is neither* A *nor* B   926 ys *deleted before* was   933 that?] MS that.

IV. i]   *RESPUBLICA.*   33

    Now my goddamighties as I dyd hither tugg youe
    So will I on my backe to your lodging lugg youe   952
    And sure yf ye can be quiet there, and lye styll
    I will shortelye bring youe, moo felowes so I wyll.
    I have a good benefyce of an hunderd markes
    yt is smale policie to give suche to greate clerkes   956
    they will take no benefice but thei muste have all,
    A bare clerke canne bee content with a lyving smale.
    Therefore sir Iohn lacke latten my frende shall have myne
    And of hym maie I ferme yt for eyght powndes or nyne   960
    The reste maie I reserve to myselfe for myne owne share
    For wee are good feeders of the poore so wee are,
    And we patrones are bounde to see (I dooe youe tell)
    The churche patrimonie to bee bestowyd well.   964
    other od corners besydes these I have mannye,
    which withall goodspeede shall encreace your co⟨mpaignie.⟩
    Come on nowe therefore: In feith I doo greate wronge   967
    to promise youe lodging, *and* kepe youe thens so long.   *exeat.*

Actus quarti scena prima.

Respublica.

Respub. O, lorde what maie yt meane to bee thus borne in hand
    And yet none emendement to fele nor vnderstand?
    people dothe dailie and hourelye to me resorte,
    Chalenging my promise of relief and comforte.   972
    I reporte to hym, as my rewlers doe to mee,
    people still affirmeth that they devourers bee.
    The more I doo hym chere/ the more he dothe dispaire,
    I saie his wealth doeth mende, he saithe it dooeth appaire. 976
    what shoulde I iudge of this? maie yt bee credible,
    or by anie reason maye yt be possible,
    that suche fowre as those in whome I have putt my truste
    shewing suche face of frendship, shoulde bee men vniuste? 980
    I will knowe if people feele yet anye redresse,

---

960 of] *possibly error for* to   966 compaignie.] *parts of the letters* mpaign *remain.*   967 g *deleted before* wronge   970 *A detached letter deleted before* nor   vnderstand?] MS vnderstand.

of his former sors *and* of hys rufull distresse.
we shall meete soone, I doubte not, *and* talke to gether.
Intrat people.
And loe as I woulde wishe, he approcheth hether.   984

Actus quarti scena secunda.
Respublica.   People.

Respub. well mette people, what place goe ye nowe vntoo?
Peopl. I cham at the ferthest to zee how yowe doo.
    we twayne must eft[1] whiles come fisike either other,
    vor wee beethe yo*ur* children, and youe beethe our mother. 988
Respublica. And howe doo youe mend now in yo*ur* thrifte *and* your purse?   F. 374ᵃ
people. As zoure ale in sommer, that is still wurse *and* wurse.
Respub. People, what sholde I saie?   *peopl.* nai masse Iscannot tell
    but we ignorams all woulde faine ye shoulde doe well.   992
    and how fele youe yo*ur*selfe? better then ye dyd, trowe?
Respub. Till god send bett*er* happe rather decaie then growe.
    this bringeth me in a conceipte of zelousye.
    Rather than muche good, woulde I speake with policie.   996
peopl. was not he drownde trowe last yeare, whan conscience was?
Respub. I see hym yond*er* appere: this cometh well to passe.
Peopl. Is thissame he?   *Resp.* yea.   *peopl.* an iche heard not you zo zai
    Choulde zware a had bee deade, orels cleane renne awaye. 1000

Actus quarti scena tertia.
⟨Avarice.⟩   Respublica.   People.

Avar. O mooste noble ladie, that I have not of late,
    Made to youe relacion how ye stande in state,
    hath not been of negligence nor to weo[r]ke by stelthe

---
                    [1] MS est

990 wurse.] MS wurse?   995 zelousye] *Brandl conj.* jelousie *mistakenly*.   997 was?] MS was   1000 awaye.] MS awaye?   1001 head. *Avarice*] a slight trace of *A* and recognizable traces of *rice* remain.   1002 state,] MS state?   1003 weorke] *emend. Magnus: Brandl emend.* werke

IV. iii] *RESPUBLICA.* 35

  but of my depe studies devising for yo*ur* wealthe. 1004
Respub. To heare the truthe thereof, I wisshed youe to see.
People. Dooeth youe studd yo*ur* braines mace Ientman, praie youe
    tell me
  for our ladie Rice puddingcakes comoditee?
Avar. I devyse what I canne for the prospiritee 1008
  of thys Ladie Respu[b]lica/ *and* hyr people.
Peopl. That lye, ere this is flowen as ferre hens as polle steple.
  Ispraie god ye studde not, as cha hard of zome elfes,
  that studdie for the comon profytte of theire owne selfes. 1012
Avar. To studie for bothe yo*ur* welthes I am a debter.
peopl. vaye than as goode ner a whitt as ner the bett*er*.
Avar. I doo nothing but coumpace therefore withowte doubte.
peopl. I vey then the vet to ferre a coumpace abowte. 1016
  vor zome good might ha bee doone in all this season.
Avar. So there is, if to p*er*ceve ytt, ye had reason.
Respub. Truelie I fele miselfe hitherto wurse and wurse.
people. And Isvele the same bothe in my grownde and my
    purse.
  vive or zixe yeare ago chad vowre kine to my paile 1021
  and att this p*re*zent houre cham scarce woorthe a good cowe
    taile
  and that tyme chad a widge, and hir vole/ *and* tenne shepe
  Nowe Iscan geate nothing my zelfe and my wife to kepe. F.374ᵇ
  Than an chad I bee with the king*es* masse counstable, 1025
  Choulde zette myselfe voorth p*er*telye, *and* zo chwas hable.
  Now vor lacke of a sallet whan my lyege hath neade
  cham vaine to take an hatte of godsgood on my heade. 1028
  And vor god my dame, this ys but small amendement.
  Iscomporte me to youe: how thinketh youre iudgement?
  Coumpacing ka? Ientman, call ye thissame coumpacing? 1031
  And/ whom shall we twaine thanke, youe, for this coumpacinge?
Avar. No sir. *peop.* Nowe by the compace that god coumpaced—
Respub. Blame have thei of god *and* man, *that* this hath coum-
    paced.

  1005 To *written over* The 1007 for] f *written over* y 1011
studde] e *added.* 1016 vet] *i.e.* fct: *Drundl emend.* vent *mistakenly.*
1022-3 *In MS these lines stand in the reverse order and are marked for transposition by the letters* .b. *and* .a. *prefixed.* 1023 *Brandl accidentally omitted* shepe *and conjectured* nete *for* tenne 1033 coumpaced—] MS coumpaced

Peopl. Asmall coumpace more nowe maie zoone coumpace by
  throod
  To make fowertie thowsaunde volk*es* heare growe throughe
  their hood. 1036
Avar. That is their owen faulte, not the faulte of policie.
Respub. God above he knowith whose faulte it is *and* n⟨ot I.⟩
Peopl. but didnot yche daylie geve youe warni*ng*? *Resp.*
  doubtelesse.
peopl. And dydnot iche plaine me to youe? *Resp.* I graunte no
  lesse. 1040
peopl. And whan ich made my mone/ what woulde [ye] to me
  tell?
Respub. as my hope was, that att length althing shoulde bee well.
peopl. Coumpacing ka? *Resp.* people I put truste in other.
peopl. valse bezeivers of zemlitee by godds mother. 1044
Avar. well suffer me then for my declaracion
  to fett Authoritee and Reformacion
  that ye maie bothe heare *and* charge them as well as me.
Respub. with[1] all my harte goode policie, let ytt so bee. 1048
  I praie youe call theim hither, if thei maie bee gotte.
people. Anche heare om, Iscan tell where thei saie true or not.

Actus quarti scena quarta.

Avarice. Insolence. Respublica. Oppression. People.

Avar. The fowlest open mowthed whretch *that* eare ye harde.
Insol. Couldest thowe by no meanes make the peasaunte afearde?
Avar. No, but anon I trowe we shall his masship trym 1053
  Conveighe hir awaie/ *and* than all wee three chide hym.
  But whiste and come apace. *Respub.* I here policies voyce.
Avar. That I mette youe so well, I doe muche reioyce. 1056
  Ladye Respublica woulde youe come hir before. F. 375ᵃ
Insolence. Madame god ye save. *Oppr. and* preserve for ever-
  more.

[1] MS will

1038 not I.] *recognizable traces of the damaged letters remain.* 1039 warning?] MS warning.   1041 ye to] *emend. Magnus; Brandl emend.* ye (*in
place of* to)   1044 zemlitee] *or less probably* zembitee   1048 with]
emend. Brandl, Magnus.   1052 afearde?] MS afearde

IV. iv]   RESPUBLICA.   37

Resp. This is happie, happe. ye come soosoone tigither.   1059
Avar. As I went, I mette them bothe twaine hasting hether.
Resp. Never in better tyme. *Insol.* Madame what is your will?
Oppress. Is there eni thing, *that* youe woulde saie vs vntill?
Respub. People cryeth owte *and* I am muche agrieved
   that we fele oure selves in nothing yet relived.   1064
Oppr. No? that is not true. Mannie declare I canne—
Respub. Even in briefe woordes/ I praie youe doe yt than.
peopl. Praie youe lett me spose with thissame new come gentman.
Insol. No sir. *Peopl.* masse but chil speake anche can spie my
   tyme whan.
Oppr. Firste youre priestes *and* bisshops have not as thei have
   had.
Resp. ⟨whan they⟩ had theire lyvinges men were bothe fedde and
   cladde.   1070
Oppress. yea, but they ought not by scripture to be calde lordes.
Respub. That thei rewle the churche with scripture well accordes.
oppr. Thei were prowde and covetous/ *and* tooke muche vppon
   theim.   1073
people. but they were not covetous that tooke all from theym.
oppr. The coigne eke is chaunged. *pepl.* yea from zillver to
   drosse,
   (twas tolde vs) vor the beste: but poore wee bare the losse.
   whan chad with zwette of browes got vp a fewe smale crumes
   att paiing of my debtes ich coulde not make my sommes.   1078
   my landlorde vor my corne/ paide me zuche sommes *and* zuche
   whan he should hate vor rent, yt was but haulfe zo muche.
   zix pence in eche shilling was I strike quite awaie
   zo vor one piece iche tooke, chawas vaine to paie him twaie.
   one woulde thinke twer brasse, *and* zorowe have I els,
   But ichwin mooste parte ont was made of our olde bells.   1084
Insol. yet if ye marke ytt well, for one peice ye have three,
   whiche for your people is no smale Commoditie.
Peop. well I nill medle in thissame matier no more,
   but Isrecke not an twer ziluer as twas avor.   1088

    1059 tigither.] MS tigither?   1061 will?] MS will.   1065 canne—]
MS canne.   1068 whan.] MS whan?   1069 and] *Brandl emend.* or
1070 whan they] *traces of* wh *remain, and most of* they   1076 losse.] MS
losse?   1079 Second zuche *interlined above a deleted word, possibly* houses

Oppr. People, ye shall att lengthe finde ytt all for the best.
People. Cha harde our parrishe clarke saye, *diuum este, Iusllum weste.*
Respub. vndoubtedly I fele many things are amisse. 1091
People. Yea Iscan tell moo things yet, an me luste by Iisse. F.375ᵇ
thei have all the woodes throughout the realme destroyed,
which might have served long yeares beeing well emploied.
and than the greate cobbes have zo take the reste to hire
that poore volke cannot gett a sticke to make a fire. 1096
Than their great grazing hath made fleshe so dere I wotte
that poore volke att shambles cannot bestowe their grotte.
Resp. I lamente yt people. Alac, what maie I doe?
I miselfe I feare shall come to ruine toe. 1100
Policie, what coumforte? whan will youe ease my smarte?
Avar. ye are as safe even nowe, but for your false harte,
As any ladie of your name in Christendome.
Peopl. If iche had zo zaide, chad lied by my holidome. 1104
Resp. ye heare what people saith which feleth as I doe.
Avar. But rude peples words will ye geve credyte vnto?
will ye iudge yourselfe after his foolishe ian⟨gling?⟩
ye wer well enoughe tyll he begonne his wrangling. 1108
Insol. will ye beleve people that hath no manier of skill
to iudge or to descerne what thing is good or yll?
he is so headstrong he muste bee bridled with Lawes.
Peopl. Thoughe zome bee starke bedlems, yet wise volkes beeth
no dawes. 1112
Insol. we have ofte founde people / mooste disobedient,
to orders mooste requisyte and expedient.
who suche a mainteynour of wrong opinions
As people in all Countries and dominions? 1116
ye oughte therefore to rebuke hym att all houres
for discouraginge anie ministers of yours.
oppr. ye muste tarrye¹ tyme ere we can your pourpose serve.

---

¹ MS turrie

1092 The speaker's name was first written at the foot of the previous page and then deleted and repeated here. 1099 doe?] MS doe. 1101 smarte?] MS smarte. 1107 iangling?] *the tails of the g's and perhaps the top of the ? remain.* 1119 youe *deleted before* we

IV. iv] *RESPUBLICA.* 39

peopl. ye *and* than while the grasse shall growe, the horse shall
    sterve.   1120
Insol. Doe ye not see this by all experience plaine
    that men from deseases recover[ed] againe,
    doe after sycknes paste/ remaine a long tyme weake?
Respub. People, herke, Authoritee dooth good reason speake.
Insol. So ye, thoughe Oppressed with Longe adu*er*sitee,   1125
    yet doubtenot are towarde wealth *and* p*r*ospiritee.
Respub. Loe people, to hope a while longer shall bee best.
peopl. well, then[1] cham p*er*swaged to doo att yo*ur* enquest.
Insol. Madame mistruste not vs yo*ur* painfull ministers.
Avar. Never had Ladie more watchefull officers.
Oppr. For my parte I will sware the gosspell booke vppon   F.376ᵃ
    That if the Lawes I have made shoulde everye one   1132
    Redowne to myne owne singuler comodytee,
    theye coulde not be frendelier framed then thei bee.
Insol. Therefore repose yo*ur*selfe madame a while *and* winke
    ye are in better case towarde then youe can thinke.   1136
Avar. we shall heare remaine, and geve people good counsaile
    quiet for to be tyll policie maie prevaile.
Resp. he will doe well with y*our* goode informacions.
Peopl. yea, vei, chil volowe their goode exaltacions.   1140
Respub. Than I leave youe all heare to god. I will dep*ar*te.
                                         exeat Resp.
people. Now howe, destructions to membre in my harte.
Avar. destructions? ye miser. *Insol.* ye peasaunt. *Oppr.* ye
    lowte.
Insol. ⟨Canne ye na⟩ught els doe but rage, *and* rave, *and* crye
    owt?   1144
Oppr. And cannot tell on whome? *Avar.* no more then can
    adawe.
Oppr. Crow against y*our* betters. *Insol. and* murmoure against
    the lawe.
    leate me heare thee prate as thow haste doone hearetofore.
Avar. Or trouble ladie Respublica anie more.   1148

---

                    [1] MS them

    1122 recovered] *emend. Brandl.*   1123 weake?] MS weake.   1128
then] *emend. Brandl.*   1144 Canne ye naught] *recognizable traces remain
of the damaged letters except the first* a *and tho* ye *and the last* n

Oppr. Thow canst not see thow wretch / canst thow? whan thow
arte well.
Avar. Ist p*a*rte of thie plaie w*i*th suche highe matiers to mell?
Insol. Doethe yt become the to barke / w*i*th suche awide throte?
Avar. And to have an ore in everye bodies bote? 1152
Insol. If thowe dooe so againe, yt shall w*i*th the bee wurse.
Oppr. we shall wring *and* pinche the / bothe by bealie *and* purse. 1154
Insol. I wolde aduise youe frende to grunte *and* grone no more.
Oppr. Doe the like againe *and* thoue shalte rue yt ful sore.
Avar. It were best for youe freend all mourmouringe to cease.
people. bum vei than chil een goo home, and vaire holde mi peace.
Insol. Dooe soo by my reade / *and* fall to honest laboure. 1159
Avar. hens home *and* bee quiete, *and* thow shalte fynde favo*ur*.
people. Then chil byd youe vare well. *Oppr.* no woord*es* but hens
a pace.
this was doone as shoulde bee. *Avar.* this was doone in right place.
people. but howe, one worde erche goe / yele geve volk*es* leave to
thinke?
Oppr. No marie will we not, nor to looke but winke. 1164
people. yes by gisse but chil loe, naie hoe thare, ħought is free,
and a catt ħey zaith maie looke on a king p*a*rdee. *exeat.*
Inso. Nowe where doo wee bee come? I home. *exeat.* *oppr.* And
I abrode. *exeat.* F. 376ᵇ
Avar. And I must see what feete abought my doore have trodde.
exeat.

Actus quinti scena prima.

Misericordia.

Miserico. wherein apeareth the graciousnesse of god
more then ynfinitelye to excede mans goodnesse,
but that he kepeth backe the sharpe stroke of hys rod
whan man woulde rage in mooste furious woodenes? 1172

Scarce anie emendes maie mannes eagrenesse appeace,
yea *and* thoughe he forgeve, he wilnot soone forgette:
towar*des* true penitens gods wrathe foorthwith doothe cease,
and he their past sinnes, behind his backe dooeth sett. 1176

1149 thow?] MS thow   1151 throte?] MS throte   1172 woodenes?]
MS woodenes

Of long sufferaunce he is with weaknesse to beare,
while anie hope of emendment dooethe Remaine
and thoughe he plague synners to call them ⟨home by⟩ feare
yet his mercye and grace are ai readie againe.   1180

His grievous displeasure dureth not for ever,
And why? quia miserationes eius,
whiche to shewe he chieflye delighteth ever,
manent super omnia Opera eius/   1184

It grieveth hym sore when he muste neades take veaungeaunce
his delite and glorie ys mercie to practyse
his tender compassion on treue repentaunce,
he hath still from the beginninge sowte texcercise.   1188

The masse of this worlde in his mercie did he frame,
the skie, yearthe, and sea his mercye replenished,
In his mercye dyd he after redeame the same
whan els remedilesse yt must have peryshed.   1192

In his mercie was Israell delivered/
from the gyptian thraldome and captivitee
In his mercye the same throughe the red sea was led
And through wildernesse to a lande of Libertee.   1196

Syth that tyme all comonweales he hath protected
and to suche as withe earnest prayer have made mone,
me Compassion he hath quickelye directed
to revive and recover theym everie one.   1200

Now lastely hath he harde the mooste doulfull[1] lament
of wofull Respublica his derling mooste dere.
Therefore me Compassion with spede he hathe sent,
hir mooste sorowfull herte to recoumforte and chere.   1204

I tarrye hir commynge that I maie hir salute,   F. 377ª
and loe me thinketh I see hir appere in place,
of frendshipp devoyde/ and of succoure destitute.
I will heare hir, and than geve wordes of solace.   1208

---

[1] MS doubtfull (doubtfull, *in the sense of* apprehensive, fearful, *seems less likely, though* doulfull *for* doleful *is an unusual spelling*).

1179 home by] *recognizable traces remain of all letters except* om

Actus quinti scena secunda.

Respublica. Misericordia/ Avaryce/ Adulacion/

Respub. O lorde haste thowe for ever closed vp thine eare?
wilt thowe never more the desolates praier heare?
wilt thow styll torne awaie thy face from my distresse?
wilte thowe cleane forsake me and leave me coumfortlesse? 1212
the secret sigthes *and* sobbes *and* praiers of myne harte,
shall thei not forever thyne yeis to me co*n*verte?
I graunte that myne offenc*es* have so muche dese*r*ved,
But for whome save sinners ys thye mercie reserved? 1216
⟨thow p*r*omised⟩ so, w*hi*ch hithertoo haste been iuste.
Despaire lorde I wilnot/ nor thie goodnesse mistruste.
Lo downe on my destresse and for thye glorie sake,
thoughe I bee ill worthie/ yet[1] mercye on me take. 1220
Miseric. Now will I speake to hir. *Resp.* who maketh me afearde?
Miser. No, I will thee comforte: god hath thi praier harde.
and now Respublica bee of good hope and truste.
Respub. O lorde nowe doe I see that thowe arte ever iuste.
Miseric. I am sent to recoumforte thee Respublica. 1225
Respub. O Ladie Compassion, Misericordia.
Miser. what saie ye to me? what wooman, can ye not speake?
I am com downe, all youre sorowes at ons to breake. 1228
Speake, wooman— *Respub.* Misericor[dia]. *Mia.* owte comfortablye
ye shall have nowe no more cause to speake desperablie.
Respub. My harte in godds mercie is so delated,
That my veraie spirite to heaven is elated. 1232
O Ladie Compassion, welcome verament
Ever bee god praysed/ *that* youe to me hathe sent.
Miseric. Now that I have put youe in sure hope of reliefe,

---

[1] MS it (*the alternative*, worthie it/ (*implied by Brandl and Magnus*), *seems less likely:* yet *could easily be miswritten or misread as* yt).

1217 thow promised] *recognizable traces remain of* h *and* p *and* s *and* d (*Brandl attempted no restoration; Magnus's* thow reservest it *is not possible*). 1220 yet] *emend. ed.* (*Brandl and Magnus print* worthie/it,). 1222–3 These two lines are written in the space left for one. 1229 wooman—] MS woman./ Misericordia.] *emend. ed.*

V. ii]   RESPUBLICA.   43

   I muste goe fett veritee to trye owte all yo*ur* griefe.   1236
   veritee shall open how yo*ur* decaie hath growne
   and then the causers thereof shalbe over throwne.
Respub. who bee the causers thereof I cannot descerne,
   but yond cometh one of them, *that* doe me governe.   1240
Miseric. what is his name? *Resp.* Policie. *Miser.* policie is goode
   he dooeth worke youe manie good thing*es* of likelihood.   F.377^b
Avar. A vengeaunce vpon hym *and* god geve hym his curse
   I am besieged nowe of everye cutpurse.   1244
   I can goe no where now in citie neither Towne
   But piers piekpurse, plaieth att organes vnd*er* my gowne.
Miseric. what talketh he? *Avar.* who speaketh yond? Res-publica?
Respub. What of the piekpurse? *Avar.* Forsouth dame Res-publica   1248
   I saide an we had twoo pielouries mo twer ner the wurse
   for yt is a light thing nowe to mete piers piekpurse.
   god p*r*eserve youe right faire Ladie *and* christe youe save
   who are yowe? *and* what woulde ye in this countrie have?   1252
Respub. Thissame is the Ladie Misericordia
   sent from god purposely. *Avar.* vnto youe Respublica?
Misericor. yea. *Avar.* Than muste ye nedes bee mooste hartelie welcome
   we had ner more nede of youe by my hol⟨ydom⟩e.   1256
   there bee in this countrye w*h*ich but ye coumforte ⟨send⟩
   are full like to make bothe a madde, *and* a shorte end.
*Miseric.*¹ I will goe to doo that I said Respublica   1259
   and retourne with spede. *Respub.* Swete Misericordia.
                                        exeat Mia.
Avar. Good Misericordia now/ and ladie mooste deare.
   Christe blister on yo*ur* harte; what make youe heare?
Respub. Come backe policie. *Avar.* I come. *Resp.* whither woulde ye nowe?
Avar. Conveigh miselfe hens honestlye, if I wiste howe.   1264

—————

                ¹ MS *Niseric.*

  1256 hulydome] *traces of the damaged letters remain, but only the* d *is recognizable.*   1257 send] *traces of* s *and* d *alone remain.*   1259 *Miseric.*] *emend.* Magnus.   1264 howe.] MS howe?

Respub. whan come ye policie? what looke ye? something loste?
Avar. Anon. If I tarie, yt will tourne to my coste.
Resp. Ah frende policie.   *Avar.* yea.   *Resp.* Now shall I bee in
   blisse   1267
   thank*es* to god.   *Avar.* we must finde p*r*ovision for this.
Respub. hah?   *Avar.* dydnot I er tell youe *that* god woulde youe
   save?
   yee maie see nowe what it is goode rewlers to have.   1270
Respublica. ye saie trewth, but looke yond*er* cometh honestie.
Avar. Praie god Amen.   *Resp.* yes looke els.   *Avar.* what newes
   bringeth he?
Adul. I shoulde speake a woorde in theare of policie.
   If I maie not so, I will speake ytt openlie.
Resp. I have not seen youe a greate while honestie.   1275
Adulac. O Noble Ladie Respublica, well yowe bee.
Respub. All shalbee now, such newes I have to me brought.
Adulac. I heare yt toulde for trouth.   Policye, all wilbee
   nought/   F. 378ᵃ
Resp. hearest thoue anie Ioyfull newes abrode, or not?
Adul. yea, I heare certaine newes/ w*h*ich are bothe brym *and*
   hotte   1280
   there is newe stertt vp a ladye cald veritee/
Respub. Than am I all safe, and sure of prospiritee.
   how was yt spoken?   *Adul.* thus in laten grosse and blunte
   Misericordia et veritas sibi obuiauerunt,   1284
   That is, Mercye and truthe are bothe mett together/
Respub. Than will yt not bee long/ ere thei bothe come hither.
Avar. hither? how so?   *Resp.* yea bothe mercie *and* verytee.
Avar. A pestle on them bothe saving my Charitee.   1288
   but softe brother honestie/ ye might mistake ytt
   Of whiche veritee wast, trowe youe *that* thaye spake ytt?
Adul. ⟨Of the ge⟩nerall Veritee Olde tymes dawghter.
Avar. Feith they were not o*ur* frend*es* *that* firste hither brought
   hir.   1292
   olde tymes doughter? that shuttle brained tall, long man

   1266 tarie,] MS tarie?   1268 thankes to god. *Avar.* we] MS *Avar.*
thankes to god. [we (*emend. Brandl. The mark before* we *is probably intended
to shift the speaker's prefix*).   1290 ytt?] MS ytt.   1291 Of the
generall] *recognizable traces remain of all the damaged letters except the first* e
and the g

That nere standeth still/ but flyghth as fast as he canne
muche like as he swymmed or glided vppon yce?
Adul. yea.   *Resp.* for all that, of wise men, he is thought mooste
  wise.
Avar. I knowe hym, he carrieth a clocke on his heade,   1297
  A sand glasse in his hande, a diall in his foreheade.
Respub. ye saie truthe policie, the same is veraye he.
Avar. Old tyme the evisdropper? I knowe hym pardee   1300
  An Aunceint turner of houses vpside downe,
  and a comon consumer of Cytie and towne.
  Old tymes doughter (quod he?) I shrewe his naked harte,
  manie of my frendes hathe he brought to paine and smarte. 1304
  Compassion and that trueth come hither to yowe?
Respub. mercie before ye came, promised so right nowe.
Avar. It is no tyme nowe honestie to be idle.
Adul. Some thing brueth?   *Avar.* It is tyme for vs to bridle. 1308
  well goe your waies afore in all haste honestee,
  And tell reformacion and Authoritee,
  That bothe theis Ladies in all goodlye facion,
  muste bee enterteyned here in this nacion/   1312
  Madame Respublica, ist not your pleasure soo?
Respub. what els? in all the haste honestee see ye gooe.
Avar. Saie ferther, that I wolde/ we fowre anon might mete F.378b
  her, or where thei will, save in the open strete.   1316
  And here youe honestie?   *Adul.* what nowe?   *Avar.* a litell
    nere,
  provyde in anie wise that veritee come not heare,
  Let Insolence and Oppression kepe hir hens.   1319
Adul. we shall all three therein/ doe oure best diligence.
Avar. Byd them well remembre the worlde will waxe quaisie
  Some of vs erelong maie happe leape at a daisie,
  Or put owte the .i. of Misericordia,
  And withowte an .i. plaie een plaine trussing corda.   1324
                        exeat Adul.
Resp. Polycye what is it that ye talke there so Long?
Avar. I send instructions that thei maie not doe wrong.
Respub. Saide ye aught to hym, that maie not be tolde to me?

1313 soo?] MS soo.

Avar. Shoulde we with ery trifling trifle trouble ye? 1328
well then ye looke for theis twoo ladi⟨es, I am sure.⟩
Respub. I truste thei wilnot faile on me to doe theire cure.
Avar. I tolde youe ever, dyd I not? that yo*ur* welthe woulde
frame. 1331
Respub. I shall rewarde yo*ur* paines: orels I were to blame.
Avar. Than beste I goe now streght to my felowes *and* see—
Respub. That thing*es* nedefull for vs maie not vnreadie bee.
Doo soo I praie youe. *Avar.* Fare ye well Respublica
till I see youe nexte. *exeat. Resp.* Nowe Misericordia! 1336
whan shall bee thy pleasure, bring hither veritee.
Intrant Mia. et veritas.
behoulde een with the worde speaking where thei bothe bee.

Actus quinti scena tertia.

Misericordia. Veritas. Respublica.

Miseric. I dare saie Respublica thinketh the tyme long.
veritee/ who can blame hir, having endured so muche wrong?
but as meate *and* drinke *and* other bodylye foode 1341
is never founde to bee, so pleasaunte nor so goode,
As whan fretting hongre/ *and* thriste hathe pincht afore
and as health after sickenes is sweeter evermore, 1344
so after decaye *and* aduersytee overcome,[1]
welth *and* prospiritee shalbe double welcome.
Miser. How nowe Respublica? have I not been long hens? 1347
Respub. Come ye firste or Laste ye blisse me with yo*ur* p*r*esence.
Miser. As I was commaunded, I bring yowe veritee, F. 379ᵃ
to helpe youe, youre people, and theire posteritee.
veritee. Dere iewell Respublica, I dooe youe enbrace.
Resp. I thanke yo*ur* goodnesse, *and* submitte me to yo*ur* grace.
Miser. Enbrace veritee for Ever Respublica 1353

---

[1] MS evercome, (*by assimilation with* 1344).

1329 ladies, I am sure.] *traces of* es, I *and of the second* s *remain.* 1331 frame.] MS frame?   1333 see—] MS see.   1334 The line was accidentally omitted by Brandl.   1344 evermore,] MS evermore?   1345 overcome] *emend. Magnus.*

And cleve fast to hir. *Resp.* yes Misericordia.
Miser. Nowe please yt yow to declare sister veritee,
    how she maie recover hir olde prospiritee   1356
    hir hono*ur*, hir wealth, hir riches, hyr substaunce
    hir comons, hyr people, hir strength, *and* hyr puissaunce.
veritee. All this wilbee recovered in continent
    and to better state also by good governement.   1360
Respub. No ladie of my name vpon yearth I esteme
    hath had better administers then myne have been,
    ⟨Pol⟩icie, Reformacion, *and* A*u*thorite.
Miser. Thes three bee veray good. *Resp.* And thee foure[th]
    Honestee.
veritas. But what if these w*h*ich have had youe *and* yo*u*rs to
    kepe,   1365
    have been ravnyng woulves in the clothing of sheepe?
Respub. If I hard not youe verytee suche sentence geve,
    by no mans p*er*swasion I could ytt beeleve.   1368
veritee. Ah good Respublica thow haste been abused,
    whom thowe chosest are vices to be refused,
    whom thow calst *Honestee* ys Adulacion
    And he that in pretence was Reformacyon   1372
    is in dede Oppression and houge violence
    Whom thowe calst Authoritee, is prowde Insolence.
    Than he *that* was Policie, the chiefe manne of price
    In dede is moost stinking *and* filthie Avarice.   1376
    he firste enveigled thee and his purpose to frame
    Cloked eche of these vices, with a vertuous name.
Resp. Benedicite, is this a possible case?
veritee. ye shall see yt p*r*oved trewe before yo*ur* owne face
    thei shalbe convinced beefore youe one by one.   1381
Resp. O Lorde what mervail if my thriste wer well nighe gon?
    but what redresse shall I have hereof? and whan?
Miseric. Suche as maie bee mooste fitte, *and* as soone as we can.
    Iustice *and* peace are appointed to descende   1385
    thone to kepe youe quiete / theother youe to defende.
    As soone as wee fowre sisters togither shalbe mette,

    1360 governement.] MS governement?   1363 Policie] *the damaged letters are only slightly defective.*   1364 foureth] *emend. Magnus.*   1372 Reformacyon] MS Reformacyon?   1379 case?] MS case.

An[1] ordre for yo*ur* establishment shall bee sett,   F. 379ᵇ 1388
    by the eternall providence/ yt is decreed[2] soo.
Respub. O mooste mercifull lorde all prayse bee thee vnto.
Miseric. I will leave youe here with my syster veritee,
    And learne of their coming wyth all celerytee.   1392
veritee. ye nede not, For I knowe thei bee nowe veray nere
    And beholde they begynne alreadie to appeare.

Actus quinti scena quarta.

Pax.   *Iustitia.*   *Veritas.*   *Misericordia.*   *Respublica.*

peace. Nowe, ons againe in god leat vs twoo systers kisse,
    In token of oure ioynyng to make a p*er*fytte blysse.   1396
Iusticia. And nowe leate vs never bee soondred any more,
    tyll we maie Respublica perfectelye restore.
veritee. Leat vs meete theym, Sister Misericordia.
Miseric. And vnto theire sight p*re*sent Respublica.   1400
Iust. pax. All haile mooste deare systers Mercye *and* verytee,
    and all hayle Respublica, with all sincerytee.
Respub. O ye ladies celestiall, howe muche am I bounde,
    with thank*es* to fall flatte before youe on the grownde   1404
    That ye thus vouchesalve a forlorne creature
    by youre heave[n]lye p*ro*tection to recure.
Iustic. I Iustice from heaven am come youe to visytte.
pax. and I peace for ever w*i*th yowe to enhabite.   1408
Miseric. And all wee fowre Systers to thutmooste of our poure
    shall restore, establishe, and defend youre honno*ur*.
Iustic. we shall firste restore yo*ur* moste happie eastate
    and suppresse all them *that* had made youe desolate.   1412
veritee. verytee shall all trueth open as ytt ys.
Iustic. I Iustice shall redresse what er is founde amisse.
Miseric. I mercye where the membre maie recured bee
    shall temper the rigoure/ *and* slake extremitee.   1416

---

[1] MS And   [2] MS drecreed

1388 An] *emend. Brandl, Magnus.*   1389 decreed] *emend. Magnus.*
1402 all *interlined with caret.*   1406 heavenlye] *emend. Brandl, Magnus.*
1416 *comma deleted after* the *and* f *deleted before* slake

pax. I peace whan thuncurable is clene cutte awaie,
 and thyll made goode, shall flourishe for ever and aie.
Respub. And I w*h*ich cannot otherwise yo*ur* goodnes deserve,
 shall yo*ur* holsome directions dewlie observe. F. 380ᵃ
 and what yf Insolence shall come or Avarice? 1421
veritee. Detest them, abhore them, *and* refuse their s*er*vice.
 I doubte not but thei wilbe styll haunting hither
 tyll we fowre shall theim fowre take here altogither. 1424
Miseric. Nowe Sisters goe wee and Respublica with vs,
 to bee newe appareled otherwyse then thus.
Iustic. Come on Respublica with vs to wealth from wooe
 godde hathe geven vs in charge that yt muste bee soo. 1428
veritee. The blysfull renovacion ye shall reigne in
 muste from hensfoorthe nowe immediatelye begynne.
 Cantent, The mercye of god et cetera, *et exeant.*[1]

Actus quinti scena quinta.

Avarice. Adulacion.

Avar. Suche gredie covetous folke as nowe of daies been
 I trowe before these p*r*esent daies wer never seen 1432
 An honest man can goe in no place of the strete
 but he shall I thinke with an hundred beggers mete.
 geve for goddes sake, geve for Saincte Charitee
 geve for oure Ladies sake, geve for the Trenitee 1436
 Geve in the waye of yo*ur* goodspede, geve, geve, geve, geve.
 Finde we oure money in the strete doo theye beeleve?
 If I had not a speciall grace to saie naye
 I wer but vndooen emongst them in one daie. 1440
 But who cometh yond? honestee? he cometh in haste.
Adul. I seke policie. *Avar.* here boye. *Adul.* All is in waste.
Avar. howe so? *Adul.* we strive againste the streame all *that* we
 doo.
Avar. wherein? *Adul.* that veritee come not this place vntoo.

---

[1] MS *god, et exeant, & cc'*

1421 Avarice?] MS Avarice   1427 wooe] *second* o *added.*   1430 S.D.
Emend. ed.   1437 geve.] MS geve? (*perhaps for* geve!).   1441 comest
deleted before the second cometh   haste.] MS haste?   1443 That
deleted before the first we   4144 wherein?] MS wherein.

For wotte ye what? *Avar.* I shall whan ye¹ have spake the
woorde. 1445
Adul. Iustice *and* peace too with full consent and accorde
are come downe from heaven/ *and* have kyste together.
Avar. God geve grace that theye twayne also come not hither.
Adulac. As mercye and trueth sibi obviaverunt 1449
So Iusticia et pax osculatæ sunt.
Avar. Is yt trewe? are theye come? *Adul.* and have kist to-
gether. F. 380ᵇ
Avar. Than carrye yn a pace for feare of fowle weather. 1452
have they kyssed together? *Adul.* yea. *Avar.* what nedeth
that?
men shoulde kysse woomen. And what poincte bee theye
att?
Adul. All the foure sisters I doo you tunderstaunde
have alreadie taken Respublica in hand 1456
Theye fowre progresse with hir in everye border,
and marre all that ever we have sette in order.
Avar. And what doeth Insolence/ or what saieth he to that?
Adul. he stampeth, he stareth, *and* snuffeth sore theareat. 1460
Avar. I advise hym to storme, *and* to shewe himselfe stowte,
thei bee weemen and perchaunce maye bee faced owte,
And peace is an honest Ladie and a quiete.
Adul. veritee and Iustice are not for oure dyete. 1464
Avar. Then mercye ys a goode one. I like hir well.
Adul. yet oft turnth she hyr face awaie, and willnot mell.
Avar. well, fall backe, fall edge, I am ons att a poincte
If Respublica come taduenture a Ioyncte. 1468
Adul. She is freshe and gaye/ *and* flourissheth who but she?
Avar. who brought yt to suche passe, will I tell hir, but wee?
Orels making these newe Ladies of hir werie,
wee shoulde thrihumphe *and* reigne. *Adul.* Oh never so merye.
Avar. well, goe to our Compaignie, I will remaine here 1473
I maie perhaps see dame Respublica appere.
I wilbe in hande with hir and make agoode face.

¹ MS he

1445 whan ye] *emend. ed.*   1447 haste *deleted before* have   1459
And what] w *written over* t

Adul. And what shall I doe? *Avar.* geve warning in the meane
　　space,　　　　　　　　　　　　　　　　　　　　　　　　1476
　that Insolence shrinke¹ not, but plaie the stowte man.
Adul. That I knowe he will doo, for ons I knowe he can.
Avar. And that youe all three be prest to come hether,
　whan nede shall require, we laye o*ur* heades together.　　1480
　whye arte thowe heare yet? *Adul.* I am gon withall my might.
　　　　　　　　　　　　　　　　　　　　　　　　　　exeat.
Avar. And loe where Respublica appereth in sight. *Intrat Resp.*
　She is nowe att hyr Nymphes bearing vpp hir traine.
　I will stande a syde, *and* Lysten a woorde or twaine.　　1484

Actus quinti scena sexta.　　　　F. 381ᵃ

Respublica. Avarice.

Respub. O Lorde thy mercies shall I sing evermore
　whiche dooest soo tenderlie thie hande maide restore.
　but what creature woulde suspicion have had,
　That my late administers had been men so bad?　　1488
　or who woulde have thowght theim counterfaict*es* to have been
　that had harde their woord*es*, and their countenaunce seen?
　and chieflye Avarice w*hich* dyd the matier breake?
Avar. That woorde towcheth me: now is tyme for me to speake.
Resp. I thought hym policie as iuste *and* true as stele.　　1493
Avar. I am gladde that by me ye doo suche goodnesse fele.
Respub. And that my wealth dyd growe, as it hath growne of late.
Avar. I ever tolde ye/ youe shoulde growe to this eastate.　　1496
Respub. Thowe tell me? *Avar.* yea I tolde youe soo in veraie dede:
　and highlie I reioyce yt doeth so well succede.
　And Salve² festa dies vpon youe Madame
　I am glad ye have gotte a newe robe so I am　　　　　1500
　what saincte in the callender doe we serve to daye,
　that ye bee so gorgeouslye decked and so gaye?
Resp. In reioycing that I shalbe cleane ryd of thee.

---

¹ MS skrinke　　² MS Salva

1476 doe?] MS doe.　　1477 shrinke] *emend. ed.*　　1481 yet?] MS yet.
1495 life *deleted before* wealth　　1496 tolde] ld *written over* e (*probably*).
1499 Salve] *emend. ed.*

Avar. Naie by this crosse ye shall neuer be rydde for me.
Respub. And of thy compares. *Avar.* well leate them doo as thei luste.
 I will ryde vppon Iyll myne owne mare *that* is iuste   1506
 other waies I shall doe yowe service of the beste.
Respub. Thowe wicked wretche dareste thowe with me to ieste?
Avar. what? I now see, *honores mutant mores*,
 but as semeth here, *raro in meliores*.   1510
Respub. The and all thy service I doe from me exile.
Avar. Is that the highe rewarde ye promist me ere while?
 is not this awise wooman and mynded to thrive
 That woulde me Policie owte of the countrie drive?   1514
Respub. Thee and thy complices from me I shall owte caste.
Avar. Than I praie youe paye vs, for *our* paines that are paste.
Respub. ye shalbe paide. *Avar.* ons I have doone the best I canne,
 Authorytee also he hath plaied the man,
 Reformacion, hath doen his *pa*rte I canne tell,
 If ye mystruste honestie, feith ye doo not well.   1520
 And as for Avarice he is conveighed quite   F. 381ᵇ
 I bed hym gette hym hens or I woulde hym endyte.
 I policie have made hym to plucke in his hornes,
 I sware I woulde els laie hym on prickels *and* thornes   1524
 where he shoulde take no rest neither daie nor night,
 so he had as liefe bee hanged as come in sight.
Respub. I maie saie with Iob, howe vainelye doe ye cheare me
 whan all the word*es* ye geve frome truth doeth disagree,   1528
 And with the wise man, I maie moost iustlye saye this,
 Iust[ici]a tamen non luxit in nobis.
 Orels with the *p*rophet in mooste sorowfull moode
 the fruicte of our Iustice is tourned into wormwoode.   1532
 well the best of youe is a detestable vice,
 And thow for thie *pa*rte arte mooste stinking Avarice.
Avar. Iesu when were youe wonte so foule moothed to bee,
 to geve suche niecknames? Ah in feith dame veritee   1536
 hath had youe in scooling of Late. well in gods name,

 1505 luste.] MS luste? 1514 drive?] MS drive. 1517 d *deleted after first* I 1528 s *deleted after* doeth 1530 *Iusticia*] emend. Brandl, Magnus.

I am sorie for yowe, een sorie, that ⟨I am.⟩
I wisse I have wrowte to sett youe in goode state,
and watched for that purpose / bothe earelie *and* late.   1540
And I wis if yowe woulde abyde my framynge,
and not thus to have fall to checking and blamynge,
I woulde ere long of yowe [haue] made suche carpenter weorke,
That ye shoulde have saide Policie had been a clerke   1544
Naie youe shoulde have seen, how I woulde have youe compacte.

Respub. yea, no doubte, ye woulde have doone somme great *and* fyne acte.

Avar. I woulde have browght haulfe kent into Northumberlande
and Somersett shiere should have raught to Cumberlande,   1548
Than woulde I have stretche[d] the countie of warwicke
vppon tainter hook*es*, *and* made ytt reache to Barwicke.
A pece of the Bisshoprique shoulde have come southwarde—
Tut, tut I tell yowe, I had wonderous feat*es* towarde.   1552

Respub. God hath placed me alreaddie in the best wise.
Avar. yea, but yet not haulfe so well as I coulde devise.[1]
but no force. well than I see ye will none of mee.
Respub. No. *Avar.* than ye can be content I departe from yee.
Respub. yea. *Avar.* well, yet *and* ye praie me I will tarrye still.
Respub. No. *Avar.* well speake me faire *and* woo me yet / *and* I will.   1558
Respub. No hens, avaunt. *Avar.* have I had of youe suche a clogg,
And nowe [youe] byd me avaunte *and* make me a dogg.   1560
Respub. Hens at ons. *Avar.* Naie, tut, an ye will ha vs, ha vs.
Respub. owte of my *pre*sence. *Avar.* well then ye wilnot ha vs /
Respub. No, avoide I charge the. *Avar.* than nedes depa*r*te I muste.
Adieu, in feith I woulde have servyd youe of truste /   1564
But sens Respublica hathe putt me to exile

[1] MS devisee. (*the last* e *added in error by assimilation with* 1555).

1538 I am.] *most of the* I *and slight traces of* am *remain*.   1543 haue] *emend. Brandl.*   1547 kent *interlined with caret.*   1549 stretched] *emend. Brandl.*   1554–5 These two lines are written in the space left for one.   1560 youe] *emend. Magnus (but the word may possibly be loosely supplied from* 1559).

where maye I goo kepe miselfe secrete for a while?
is there neu*er* a goode chaplaine in all this towne,
that will for a while hide me vnd*er* his gowne?   1568
Never a goode farmer? neu*er* agoode m*er*chaunte manne?
well I will goo pieke owt some corner yf I canne
but first will I monishe my fellowes of this geare,   1571
An we scape this plounge, I care not for the next yeare. *exeat.*
Respub. Nowe will I to Iustice *and* thother ladies three,
And praie that these vices maie all suppressed bee.
                                                Intrat people.
But loe, heare cometh people, I will nowe torne againe
And firste knowe of his goode state by a woorde or twaine. 1576

Actus quinti scena septima.
Respublica.   People.

Respub. what standith he prying? dareth he not entre?
people. ⟨Ch⟩oul⟨de vai⟩ne zee my ladie: but Isdare not venter.
Respub. Shrinke not backe from me, but drawe to me my deare
    frend.   1579
people. Chill virst knowe an ye bee alone zo god me mende.
Respub. Come, here bee non but thie frends, me beleve.
people. well, than chil bee zo bolde to peake in by yo*ur* leve.
Respub. how happeneth that thowe hast so long been me froo?
people. Marie chill tell yowe: as soone as ye were agoe   1584
    hither cam a zorte of courtnalls, harde men *and* zore
    Thei shaked me vp, chwas ner zo rattled avore.
    Theye vell all vppon me catche awoorde *that* might catche,
    well was hym that at me people might geat a snatche.   1588
    Choulde have been at home rather then anewe grote.
    Iche maie zedge to yowe, Isfearde pulling owte my throte.
    they bade me pieke me home, *and* come att yowe no more.
    An iche did, thei zware Isshoulde bee corroupt therefore.   1592

1568 gowne?] MS gowne.   1569 manne?] MS manne   1576 firste]
r *interlined with caret.*   knowe *repeated and deleted.*   1578 Choulde
vaine] *traces remain of all the damaged letters except the* a (*Magnus reads*
Shoulde *wrongly*).   1583 froo?] MS froo   1587 Theye] y *blotted and
doubtful.*

zo thieke prowte howrecop, what call ye hym? *Resp.* Insolence.
People. yea, even thickesame, he vaire popt me to silence.
Respub. And howe ys it with youe now? better then it was?
people. All beginneth now to come gailie well to passe.
    wee heare of your goode vortune that goeth a bowte   1597
    howe ye beeth permounted which makithe all vs proute.
    And iche am hable sens to bie me anewe cote,
    And Isthanke god chave in my purse a zilver grote.   1600
    I wis iche cowlde not zo zai these zixe yeares afore.
    who ever cawsed yt, ill thanke have they therefore/
Respub. Thei wilbe heare soone/ byde youe theim here for a traine.   F. 382^b
people. Masse but I nynnat. woulde ye have om sqwatte owt ons braine?   1604
Respub. They shallnot doe the harme the value of a poincte.
peopl. then an youe zaie the woorde ichill ieoperde a io[i]ncte.
Respub. If thei but offer thee wrong they shall smarte therefore.
people. Naie will ye bee zoo goode to tye om vp a vore?   1608
    and what shalche zai to om? *Resp.* nothing but bee a bayte
    tyll take theim all here soodainelie I maie awayte.   *exeat.*
people. well ytt shalbe doo, Choulde laugh and bothe my hands clappe,
    to zee Ricepuddingcakes envies take in a trappe.   1612
    and azee praie, if zome of om comnot yonder.
    choulde my ladie had byd ner zo lytle longer.

Actus quinti scena Octava.

Insolence.   *Adulacion.*   *Oppression.*   *Pe⟨op⟩le.*   *Avarice.*

Insol. where is Avarice howe? he doeth not nowe appere.
Adul. he bydde me monishe youe that we might all mete here.
Oppr. But see where people staundeth. *Adul.* what dothe he here now?
Oppr. Abought litle goodnes, I dare my woorde avowe.   1618

    1593 hym?] MS hym.   1615 head. *People*] recognizable traces of the damaged letters remain.   Avarice does not enter till 1631.   1618 goodnes,] MS goodnes? [*perhaps for* goodnes!].

Insolence. Let vs speake vnto hym. people wherefore *and* why,
    like a loytring losell standeste thowe heare idelye?   1620
Oppr. Thowe comest to Respublica to make some mone.
Adul. Orels some complainte.   *pepl.* youe all see cham here alone.
Insolence. ye muste have silver money muste ye ientilman?
    youe cannot be content with suche coigne as wee can.   1624
Oppr. ye¹ muste burne woode *and* cole muste ye all of pleasaunce?
    burne turves or some of thy bedstrawe with a vengeaunce.
Adul. ye muste eate freashe meate bowght from the shambles
    muste ye?
    eate garlike and Onnyons *and* rootes or grasse an luste ye.   1628
Insolence. In feith I will whippe youe for this ye peasaunte lowte.
Adul. And twygge youe.   *Insolenc.* ere an other yeare come
    abowte.
Adul. but see where Avarice cometh rennyng veraie faste.
                                                Intrat Avar.
Avar. I have trodde *and* scudde tyll my winde is almoste paste,
    yet my mates are not where.   *Insol. et Adul.* we bee heare come
    of late.   1633
Avar. Be there not trowe ye² honester men in Newgate?
Insolence. No woordes of reproche brother myne I reade
    youe.   F. 383ᵃ
Avar. None but goddigod eve, *and* goddigod spede youe.
    Fare³ ye well againe an ye bee faling owte nowe.   1637
Insol. Adul. we mynde yt not.   *Avar.* twere more neade to looke
    abowte youe.
Insol. Howe goethe all tell vs?   *Avar.* my ladye is waxte froward.
    our names bee all knowen, so there is araie towarde/ 1640
Insol. oppr. God spede vs well.   *Avar.* ons I am thruste owte of
    service.
Adul. Alas what maie I doe?   *Insol. oppr.* tell vs thie best aduise.
Ava. Naie I cannot have youe whan I woulde, none of yowe all,
    therefore shifte for your selves, eche one for me youe shall. 1644

---
            ¹ MS we   ² MS we   ³ MS Feare

    1620 idelye?] MS idelye.   1623 ientilman?] MS ientilman.   1625
ye muste] *emend. ed.*   pleasaunce?] MS pleasaunce   1627 muste ye?]
MS muste ye.   1634 ye] *emend. ed.*   Newgate?] MS Newgate.   1637
Fare] *emend. ed.*   1643 woulde,] MS woulde (*this seems the only inter-
pretation consistent with* 1644: *Brandl and Magnus put the comma after*
youe).

Adul. Naie for the pashe of god, tell vs what beste to doo,
  ye knowe I was ner slake to resorte¹ youe vntoo.
Avar. T⟨he⟩is l⟨adies⟩ that are come for comon weales reliefe,
  pr⟨ep⟩are to weorke vs woo, and doo vs all mischiefe.   1648
Insolence. Naie by his precious populorum I shwere,
  Not the prowdest of them all can hurte me a heare.
Oppre. If theye offre of vs to make theire gawdes or toyes,
  theie shall [find] I trowe, we are no babes, nor boyes.   1652
Avar. To prevaile againste them with force I doo despaire.
Insolence. Bee that as bee maie.   *Adul.* I will fall to speaking faire.
  butte of all this trouble we maie thanke people this wretche.
Oppr. Feith vilaine if wee scape, thow shalte an halter stretche.
Adulacion. But what remedie therwhile?   *Avar.* feith all wilbe nawght.   1657
Adul. Tell vs what to doo.   *Avar.* I will. thei come, wee are caught.
Adul. whether shall I renne?   *Avar.* Nowe sing a song, honestie.
Adul. I am past singing now.   *Avar.* yes one song honestie.   1660
  haye, haie, haie, haie,
  I wilbe merie while I maie.

Actus quinti scena Nona.

Veritee. Iustice. Avarice. Respublica. Adulacion.
  Mia. peace. people. Insol. Oppression.

Veritee. Heare theye bee all fower. This is an happie chaunce.
Avar. Take eche manne a ladie sirs/ *and* leate vs goo daunce.
Resp. I leafte people heare for atraine to holde them talke.
*Avar.*² Alas that I coulde tell/ wh*i*ch waie beste hens to walke.

---

¹ MS restore   ² Prefixed to 1667 in MS.

1646 resorte] *emend. ed.*   1647 Theis ladies] *recognizable traces remain of all the damaged letters.*   1648 prepare] *only a trace remains of the first e but the p is only slightly damaged: the first r has apparently been altered, and is illegible.*   1652 find] *emend. Brandl, Magnus* (*alternatives are of course possible*).   1655 of all] MS of (all   1656 wee *interlined above* ye *deleted.*   1663 head. *people. Insol. interlined with caret.*   1664 chaunce.] MS chaunce?   1666 *Avar.*] *emend. Magnus. The prefix is erroneously written at the head of the verso instead of at the foot of the recto page. The rule is after* 1665 *not* 1666.

what bee thes faire Ladies? *and* whether will theye
trowe? F. 383ᵇ
Iustice. wee arest youe sirs all fowre as ye stande in a rowe,
not so hardie in yo*ur* hart*es* oure areste to gaine saie.
Avar. Naie we are content if ye let vs gooe oure waie. 1670
Iustice. Noo not a foote, we muste firste y*our* reckeninge take.
Avar. I nere bought nor solde w*i*th yowe reckeninge to make
Nor I knowe not who yowe bee. *Iust.* Iustice is my name.
Avar. where is your dwelling? *Iust.* In heaven *and* thens I came.
Avar. Dwell ye in heaven/ *and* so madde to come hither?
all our hucking here, is howe we maie geate thither. 1676
Iustice. I bring heaven w*i*th me and make it where I am.
Avar. Than I praie youe lett me bee y*our* pr*e*ntise madame.
I wilbe at y*our* becke. *Iust.* ye shall ere ye de⟨p*ar*te.⟩ 1679
Avar. I woulde learne howe to make heaven w*i*thall my harte.
well as for Ladie Misericordia,
I remember I sawe yowe w*i*th Respublica.
Adul. youe if youe soo please maie doo muche goode in this lande
Mannie att this howre dooe nede y*our* goode helping hande. 1684
Avar. And ye cam downe from heaven too, I iudge. *Miseric.* yea
sure.
Avar. why what folke are ye *that* cannot heaven endure?
And what maie I call youe Ladie? *pax.* my name is peace.
Avar. ye have long dwelte w*i*th vs, wee have been long in
peace. 1688
peace. Cale ye it peace sirrha whan brother *and* brother,
cannot bee content to live one by an other,
whan one for his howse, for his lande, yea for his grote
is readie to strive, *and* plucke owte an others throte? 1692
I will in all suche thing*es* make p*er*fecte vnion.
Avar. Than goode night the laweiers gaine by Saincte Tronnion.
westminster hale might goo plaie if that cam to passe.
feithe we must serve youe w*i*th a Sup*er*sideas.¹ 1696
veritee. well, leave vaine pratling, *and* nowe come aunswere to
mee.

---

¹ MS Supsideus.

1677 and *interlined above* bee youre (*from* 1678) *deleted.* 1678 Than]
a (*or* e) *blotted and illegible.* 1679 departe.] *the tail of the* p *alone
remains.* 1687 Ladie?] MS Ladie.

Avar. I muste heare first what ye saie, *and* who ye bee.
veritee. I am dame veritee.   *Avar.* what? the dawghter of Tyme?
veritee. yea.   *Avar.* I knowe my m*aister*/ yo*ur* father well
   afyne.   1700
   welcome faire Ladie, swete ladie, litle ladye,   F. 384ᵃ
   plaine ladie, smoothe ladie, sometyme spittle ladye,
   Ladie longtong, ladye tell all, ladie make bate,
   and I beseche youe from whens are ye come of late?   1704
veritee. I am sproong owte of the earth.   *Avar.* what, ye doo butt
   ieste.
verytee. The booke saieth, *Veritas de terra orta est.*
Avar. happie is he w*hi*ch hathe, that garden platte I trowe
   owte of w*hi*ch suche faire blossomes doe spring *and* growe   1708
   yet this one thing I saye.   *verit.* what?   *Avar.* ye are frende to
   fewe,
   preste to open all thing*es* and mennes manniers to shewe.
veritee. If ye bee true *and* iuste that is yo*ur* benefite.
Avar. True or vntrue, iuste or vniust it is your spite,   1712
   and gladde ye are to take other folk*es* in A tryppe,
   y⟨.t.y..d..i.l....⟩we *and* than yo*ur* owne selfe on the whippe.
   well ye might bee honeste of yo*ur* tonge if yowe woulde.
veritee. If yo*ur* actes were honest ye did but as ye shoulde.   1716
Avar. who chargeth me w*i*th the cryme of anie vice?
Veritee. Thowe calst thieselfe policie, and arte Averice.
Avar. Naie I defie youre mallis, I am policie.
   Aske of my felowes here, am not I policie?   1720
veritee. Ladies, will ye all see hym openlie tried?
Iustice. if he bee an yll one, leate hym bee descryed.
veritee. what haste thow in thie bosome?   *Avar.* nothing I truelie/
veritee. Nothing trulie gotte saie.   shewe ytt foorth openlie.
Avar. what shoulde I shew foorth?   *verit. that* bag in thie bosome
   hid.   1725
Avar. It lieth well, I thanke youe as muche as thoughe I dyd.
veritee. Naie come on, owte with ytt.   *Avar.* loe here tis for yo*ur*
   fansie.

   1704 late?] MS late.   1714 *Only doubtful traces of the damaged words
   remain.   Magnus's restoration* yes, ye do it nowe *is not altogether consistent
   with what is visible (the first word was doubtless* yet *and the last probably*
   nowe).   1720 policie?] MS policie   1723 bosome?] MS bosome.
   1726 *Avar.* written over *veritee* smudged out.

verytee. Geve it me.   *Avar.* yea, naie I defie that polycye.   1728
ver. Open yt.   *Avar.* yea, that eche bodie might bee catching,
   Somes teeth I thinke water een sens to bee snatching.
ver. we muste nedes see what yt is.   *Avar.* tis abag of rie.   1731
veritee. Rye, what Rye?   *Avar.* A bag of Rie.   *ver.* suche as men
   doe eate?
Avar. A bag of Rye flowre a greate deale bett*er* then wheate.
verytee. Lett vs see what Rye ytt is, poore it owte in haste.
Avar. yea shall? I trowe not. In dede soo might wee make
   waste.   1735
veritee. There is no remedie,[1] powre ytt owte in my lappe. F.384^b
Avar. Naie if there bee no choyse I will vse myne owne cappe.
veritee. So, A bag of Rye q*uod* thoue?   *Avar.* yea so god me spede.
veritee. Thou saiest even trueth tis a bagg of Rye in dede,
   vsiree, periuree, pitcheree, patcherie,   1740
   pilferie, briberee, snatcherie, catcherie,
   Flatterie, Robberie, clowterie, botcherie,
   Troumperye, harlotrie, myserie, tretcherie.
Avar. There is too[2] an please youe, a litle sorcerie/   1744
   witcherie, bauderee, *and* suche other grosseree.
veritee. And howe gotste thowe all this in thye possession?
Avar. Pardon me, and I will make my confession.
   The worlde is harde/ *and* the bag ys but veraie smale.   1748
   I gotte it where I colde to goe on beg⟨ging wi⟩tha⟨ll,⟩
   A plaine true deling manne that loveth not to ⟨st⟩eale,
   and I durst not bee bolde to crave of comon weale.
veritee. Now doe of thie gowne, *and* tourne the inside owtwarde.
Avar. Leate me alone/ and an Angell for a rewarde.   1753
veritee. Come of atons: whan? come of. No more gawdies nor
   iapes.
Avar. muste I nedes whipp over the chaine like Iacke a napes?

---

[1] MS remodie,   [2] MS twoo

1731 A riming line appears to be missing. In place of 1732 Magnus suggests: *veritee.* Rye, what Rye? *Avar.* A bag of Rie, yea 'tis a bag of Rye. | *ver.* a bag of rie thou saiest such as men doe eate?   1744 too] *emend. ed.*   1746 possession?] MS possession   1749 begging withall,] *of the damaged letters recognizable traces remain of the first* g *and of* w *and of* ll (*the letter after the first damaged* g *looks like an* e *but there is a dot*).   1750 steale] *recognizable traces of the damaged letters remain.*   1752 *Magnus supposed the* to *stand for* thee (*mistakenly*).

Respub. owte, in the vertue of god/ what doo yee here see?
Avar. All this had been loste Respublica but for me.   1757
Resp. O lorde where hast thow dragged vp all these purses?
veritee. where he hathe had for theim manie thowsaunde curses.
Respub. where hast thowe gotten them? tell trueth *and* donot lye.
Avar. where no honest manne coulde have gotten theym but I.
   In blinde corners where some woulde have hourded theim
   had not I take theym with the manier *and* bourdened theym.
Respub. And whither was yt thine entent to conveigh theim
   now?   1764
Avar. I hidde them that I might bring theim safelie to youe.
   I durst not beare theim openlie to god I vowe,
   I wis ye have harde me blame piekepurses or nowe.
   and this is all yo*ur*s. *Verit.* It is hers in veraie dede.   1768
Avar. with Sufferaunce I coulde gette mo to helpe hir nede.
veritee. Howe saie[1] ye Respublica nowe to Policie?
Respub. I ner suspecte hym nor hadde hym in zelosie.   F. 385[a]
veritee. Een suche like counterfaict*es* shall all the rest appere.
   sirs doe of yo*ur* vtmoste robes eche one even heare.   1773
   Now what these are yee see plaine demonstration.
Respub. Insolence.   Oppression.   Adulacion.
   O lorde howe have I bee vsed these five yeres past?
people. Naie Isner thought bett*er* of om iche by godd*es* vast.
   vey madame my Ladie suche Strussioners as these   1778
   have ofte made youe beeleve the moone was a grene chese.[2]
veritee. Nowe ye see, what thei are, the punishment of this
   muste bee referred to the goddesse Nemesis
   she is the mooste highe goddesse of correccion
   Cleare of conscience *and* voide of affeccion
   she hath powre from a bove, *and* is newlie sent downe   1784
   T⟨o⟩ redr⟨esse a⟩ll owtrages in cite *and* in Towne
   she hathe powre from godde all practise to repeale
   w*hi*ch might bring Annoyaunce to ladie comonweale.
   To hir office belongeth the prowde toverthrowe/   1788

---
         [1] MS faie   [2] MS che. se

1757 mc.] MS mc?   1760 them?] MS them: 1771 suspecte] *Magnus emend.* suspected (*wrongly*).   1776 p*a*st?] MS past   1785 To redresse all] *recognizable traces remain of all the damaged letters.*   1787 comonweale.] MS comonweale?   1788 toverthrowe] w *altered and final* e *added.*

and suche to restore as iniurie hath browght lowe.
tys hir powre to forbidde *and* punishe in all eastates
all p*re*sumptuous immoderate attemptates.
hir cognisaunce therefore is a whele *and* wings to flye, 1792
in token hir rewle extendeth ferre *and* nie.
A rudder eke she bearethe in hyr other hande,
as directrie of all thing*es* in everye Lande.
than pranketh she hir elbowse owte vnd*er* hir side, 1796
to keape backe the headie *and* to temper theire pride.
To hir therefore dere sisters we muste nowe resorte,
that she maie geve sentence vppon this nawghtie sorte
She Knowith what is fyttest for theire correction 1800
Nemesis muste therefore herin geve direction.
Iustic. Than people while we ladie Nemesis doo fett
all these offendo*ur*s in thie custodie wee sett,
theim to aprehende *and* kepe tyll wee come againe. 1804
People. An ye geve me toritee chill kepe om that is plaine.
Ins. oppr. Shall people kepe vs, of whom we have been lordes?
People. Stande still, or by Iisse [chil] bynde youe vaste with chordes.
Naie, sirs iche ha youe nowe in my custoditee.
Avar. Masse, I wilbe gone for myne owne Comoditie. 1809
people. zoft whether wilte thow? nilt thowe not bee roylled? F. 385b
stande styll skitbraind theaff or thy bones shall be coilled.
yond bee thei comyng nowe che warte that will tame ye.
A zee, arte thowe gon too? come backe *and* evill a þee. 1813

*Actus quinti scena de*cima.

*Nemesis. Respub. Mia. veritas. Iustic. pax. peple.
Insol. oppr. Adulac. Avar.*

Nemesis. Come foorth Respublica o*ur* derling mooste dere.
Respub. At youre woorde mooste gracious Ladie I am here.

1795 directrie] *Magnus emend.* directrice (*but the word is not recorded till the next century*).   1796 elbowse] *written* elbowce *and the* c *altered to* s *or* ss (*but the letter is badly formed and doubtful*).   1805 Here the Ladies go out.   1807 chil] *emend. Magnus: Brandl emend.* I   1808 mine (?) *deleted before* my   custoditee] u *blotted and doubtful.*

V. x] *RESPUBLICA.* 63

Nemesis. Are these yo*ur* trustie men that had youe in govermente? 1816
people. The skitb[r]aines nold not bee roilled ner sens ye wente.
Nemesis. People whie aret thow bashefull *and* standest soo farre?
   bee of goode chere nowe, *and* I warraunte thee come ner.
people. I nill come no nere cha not bee haled vp w*i*th states, 1820
   but Iscannot bee fichaunte enoughe emongst ⟨m⟩y ⟨mates.⟩
Nemesis. Come nere whan I bydde thee. *peop.* Marye but I
   ninnat
I nam not worthye to perke w*i*th yowe no I nam not.
Nemesis. well, Respublica are these youre Late governoures,
   whom ye tooke for faithfull/ *and* trustie counsailours? 1825
Respub. yea, forsouth madame. *Avar.* These three¹ bee, but I
   am none,
for I was discharged nigh haulfe an howre agone.
Nemesis. Come firste stande foorth here, thow Adulacion.
Adul. Speake agoode woorde for me Ladie Compassion.
people. Naie, she shall not nede, I chill speake for the miselfe. 1830
   Madame take goode hede for this is a naughtie elfe.
Adul. Naie, madame the cause of all this was Avarice.
   he forged vs newe names/ and dyd vs all entice.
Oppr. wee neither dyd nor coulde weorke, but by his aduise.
Adul. Because I gotte no more he chidde me ones or twise.
Insol. Madame onlye Avarice made vs all to fall. 1836
Avar. yea? Falle to peaching?² naie, then will I tell all.
   Madame ere I had taught these m*e*rchaunt*es* enie while
   Thei were conynger then I all men to bee guile.
   And veritee sawe myne were sm*a*ll purses *and* baggs 1840
   tottering looce abought me like windshaken rags.
   but he that shoulde have bagged that Insolence dyd winne,
   Muste have made a poke to putt five or six shiers in 1843
   he muste have made wyde sack*es* for Castells, townes, *and*
      wood*es*, F. 386ª

¹ MS theree (*but the first* e *may have been deleted*). ² MS p'ching?
(*i.e.* preching?).

1816 govermente?] MS govermente   1817 skitbraines] *emend. Brandl,
Magnus.*   1821 my mates.] *recognizable traces remain of the first* m *and
slight traces of the second* m *and of* t *and* s   1837 peaching] *conj. Magnus.*

the canvesse to make them of, were woorth ten tymes my
  goodes.
Than oppression here, to feather well his neaste,
Cared not of theire Livelood whom he dispossseste.   1847
Bisshops, deanes, p*r*ovestes, ye poore folke from the spittle,
Landes w*i*th churche *and* chapple, all was for him to litle.
poore I did not soo, I scraped but lytle crummes   1850
and here and there w*i*th odde endes, patchid vp my summes.
Flatterye gotte his thrifte, by counterfaicte honestie
yet by these tenne bones, I bydde hym vse modestie
Therefore spare not hym he will ner come to goode passe
But I maie welbe mended by the marie masse.   1855
Mia. Ladie Nemesis now have yee Occasion,
And matier to shewe youre commiseracion.
⟨It⟩ is m⟨uche m⟩ore glorie *and* standith with more skyll,
Lo⟨st⟩e shepe to recover, then the scabye to spill.   1859
Iustice. But howe shall this redresse bee well p*r*osecuted,
if Iustice with mercye shalbee executed?
Streight Iustice muste suche greate enormiteis redresse,
Severitee muste putt men in feare to transgresse;
Iustice muste geve eche manne that he dothe deserve.   1864
Mia. If offendours were not, wherefore might mercye serve?
Avarice. Stike harde to it goode shwete Ladie Compassion
we are els vndoone/ by cock*es* bytt*er* passion.
Mia. Veritee how saie youe? have I not spoken well?   1868
veritee. mercie in one place w*i*th Iustice sometyme maie dwell,
and right well agree togither.   howe saie youe peace?
pax. where althing is well emended I doo encreace/   1871
Nemesis. Ladies we have harde all yo*ur* descrete aduises/
a*n*d eche one shall have some p*ar*te of youre devises/
neither all nor none, shall taste of severitee/
But as theye are nowe knowen throughe ladie veritee/
so shall theye receyve oure mercie or o*ur* Ire,   1876
As the wealthe of Respublica shall best require.

1848 ye] (*i.e.* yea) *Magnus emend.* þe (*but* þ *is only used in People's part*).
1858 It is muche more] *of the damaged letters recognized traces of* It *and* h
and m *remain.*   1859 Loste] *only the tops of the letters are damaged.*
1860 prosecuted] *the scribe first wrote* p̱ (*i.e.* per) *and then added the curl for* p̱
(*i.e.* pro): *Brandl read* prosecuted *and Magnus* persecuted   1861 executed?] MS executed.   1865 serve?] MS serve.   1870 peace?] MS peace.

Now Adulacion what saieth youe in this case?
Adulac. Nought in myne excuse, but submitte me to your grace.
onelie this I promise if I maie mercye fynde, 1880
vtterlie for ever to chaunge my wicked mynde.
I nere sought afore myne owne private gayne so muche,
But I will ferther Commonweales tenne tymes so muche.
Nemesis. well thowe maiest become a worthie subiecte yt ys
plaine. F. 386ᵇ 1884
Adul. Els ye knowe at all tymes howe to reache me againe.
Nemesis. Thowe mightest swerve of frailtee, thow mightst doo
too please,
Thow mightst doo for feare/ thow mightst doo too lyve in ease.
well vppon thie promyse for ons wee pardon thee; 1888
Goo, *and* see that from hensfoorthe thow bee perfeicte honestee.
Adulac. So long as shall please god to geve me life and heale
I shall mooste duelie serve god *and* the Commonweale.
Avar. Nowe to thee Avarice have att thye petticote. 1892
Nemesis. Now the plague of Comonweales as all men doo note,
Come foorth Avarice: to spare thee wilbe no boote,
thow muste bee plucked vpp een bye the veraie roote
because thowe scrapedst vp what ever thow mightst geate.
Avar. In dede I thanke god there is no man in my ⟨debte.⟩
Nemesis. And because thowe caughtst yt, by wrong contribu-
cion 1898
thowe shalte firste *and* formooste make restitucion.
Avar. Leat me than with pardon goe hens abowte yt lightlye.
Nemesis. No ye shall have helpe to see it doon vprightlie.
people take this felowe— *Avar.* godde save me from this
plounge.
Nemesis. That he maie bee pressed, as men doo presse a spounge
that he maie droppe ought teverye man hys lotte, 1904
to the vtmooste ferthing that he hath falslie gotte.
peopl. An ye bydde mee chill squease hym as drie as A kyxe.
Avar. Naye the pashe of godde I shall then die of the flixe.
Nemesis. Naie, thowe shalte deliver hym to the hedd Officer
which hathe Authoritee Iustice to mynister. 1909

1881 mynde.] MS mynde? 1887 feare *deleted before* for 1891
duelie] d *written over* s 1897 debte] *the first three letters are clear; only
traces remain of the others.* 1902 felowe—] MS felowe.

people. Chil lyver hym to the Counstable *and* come againe.
Nemesis. Now Iustice for these twoo *that* doe here remaine
   because the faulte of Insolence is hainous *and* greate
   Lucifers owne faulte taspire to the highest seate
   And beecause Oppression hath wronged men so sore   1914
   That he spoiled innocent*es* of all thei had and more,
   people shall deliver them vnto safe costodie
   where thei maie no farther anoye anie bodie
   whan the tyme maie serve/ texamine *and* trie their cause,
   Call them bothe before youe, *and* Iudge them by the lawse. 1919
people. And shalche carrie awaie these same twoo men also?
Nemesis. yea goe deliver them to an officer goe.   F. 387ª
   Now dearling Respublica ye are in tholde goode eastate
   and they taken awaie that spoiled youe of Late.
   Nowe cleve to these Ladies from heaven to youe directe   1924
   they from all corruption will youe safe p*r*otecte.
   well I muste goe hens to an other count[r]eye nowe
   that hathe of redresse the like case *that* was in youe.
   I leave youe for thys tyme immortall thank*es* to geve   1928
   to godde and yo*ur* Soveraigne w*hi*ch doo youe thus relieve/
Resp. Thankes be to thee O lorde w*hi*ch haste this worlde wrowght,
   and hast me too this state from vtter Ruine brought.   1931
Pax. Now leat vs all togither bothe with harte *and* voice,
   In god and in Quene Marie mooste ioyfullie reioyce.
veritee. Praying that hir Reigne mooste graciouslye begonne
   ⟨Maie long⟩ yeares endure as hithertoo yt hath doone.
Mia. Praie wee forre hir Counsaile to have long life *and* healthe.   1936
Iustice. Theire soveraigne to serve.   *pax.* And to mainteine Comonwealthe.
om*nes.*   Amen.
Cantent/ et exeant.
Finis.

1915 *A letter (possibly* t) *deleted before* and   more,] MS more?
1926 countreye] *emend. Magnus.*   1935 Maie long] *slight traces remain of* M *and* l *and recognizable traces of* ong

GLOSSARY

A number of proverbial sayings and expressions not strictly glossarial are included for the sake of record. So are quotations. Words and phrases peculiar to People's part are starred. His speech is a mixture of would-be comic perversions and conventional stage-dialect of a south-western type. Among its more prominent features is the anomalous use or lack of concord of verbal forms (such as youe liest ... youe arte, 638–9), but these do not conveniently admit of glossarial treatment. Nor, as a rule, have the normal substitutions of v for f and z for s been admitted. In the text the often anomalous word-division of the original has been preserved, and in general the glossary follows the text.

A

a, at, 437.
a, he, 'a chive', he shall attain (*but perh. a miswriting for* achive), 140; *also* *683, 1000.
*abee, he be, 705.
abought, about, 1168, 1618; in pursuit of, 899.
abusion, abuse, deceit, 24.
accordyd, agreed, determined, 216.
Acyons, ? Asians, Asiatics, 409.
administer, administrator, governor, 585; administers, 1488.
aduises, opinions, counsels, 1872 (*the plural is rare*).
*afore, before this, past, 1602.
afyne, to the end, completely (*little more than intensive*), 1700 (*no quots. in O.E.D. after* 1460).
against, 'een as a. suche a thing', ? at the very thought of it, 157.
againste, *conj.*, against *or* in preparation for the time (when *or* of), 416, 791. (*Magnus glosses* 416 *as* again (*a very rare use,* O.E.D. *sense* C) *but the meaning is clear from* 433.)
agoe, a goe, *for* agone, *past part. of* ago, to go, 239, 1584.
agone, ago, 366.
agrieved, grieved, afflicted, 1063.
ait aio ... negat nego, 'he sais, I say ... he denies, I deny'; one prepared always to agree with another, a yes-man, 186.
albes (thalbes), albs, surplices, 871.
*alese dicts, *for* alias dicta, 637.

all, altogether, entirely, 1282.
all that we doo, for all we can do, 1443.
all thing(e), 110, 455, 479, 608, &c.; (althing) 1042, 1871; everything.
alone, a lone, unique, unrivalled, 82, 766.
amaigne, amain, immediately, 342.
amices, folded linen scarves, 871.
amonges, amongst, 273.
an, if, 174, 259.
*anche, an che, if I, 1050, 1068.
and (&), an, if, 1557.
angell, an angel-noble (*worth at the time* 10s.), 1753.
annoyaunce, molestation, injury, 1787.
appaire, grow worse, decay, 976.
appeace, appease, satisfy, 1173.
applye, adapt themselves, comply, 818.
appropriacions, benefices, tithes, 808.
aprehende, arrest, hold in custody, 1804.
araie, array, position of affairs, trouble, 1640.
aret (thow), art (thou), 1818 (*perh. a miswriting*).
armes, by his, by God's arms, 128.
armes (tharmes) of Callis, the arms of Calais, 782.
as, such as, who, 264.
*as goode ner a whitt as ner the better, as well do nothing as nothing profitable, 1014.
assaille (tassaille), to accost, attempt, 251.

GLOSSARY

as true as stele, 1493.
atons, at once, 1754.
atraine, for, for a train (q.v.).
att, to, 262; *? for, towards, 1078; ? with, attended by, 1483.
attemptates, attempts, outrages, 1791.
aungelots, angelets, little angels (*coins worth half an angel*), 767.
avoide, depart, 1563.
*****a vore,** beforehand, first, 1608.
avowe, my woorde, pledge my word, 1618.
awayte, to lie in wait, plan, 1610.
*****azee,** 1613, **a zee,** 1813, see, look.

B

bagged, put in a bag, 1842.
ball, *app. a dog's name,* 313.
bard, barred, excluded, kept away, 490.
bare, naked, unprovided, 891.
barke, to cry out, find fault, 1151.
barking, outcry, 870.
bate, discord, strife, 1703.
battaile, make a, be at odds, 896.
bauderee, bawdry, procuring, 1745.
bayte, bait, enticement, 1609.
*****be,** by, 'b. triall', on trial, 713.
bealie, belly, 756, 1154.
beare faire in hand(e), to deal courteously with, 680, 941; *cf.* borne in hand.
beaste, 'a verye b.', a mere ass, 782, 'be a b.', have no more sense than a beast, 87.
bed, bade, 1522.
*****bedlems,** madmen, 1112.
bee, been, 1017, 1025, 1776, 1820.
bee come, become, betake oneself, 1167.
*****beeleve the moone was a grene chese,** 1779.
been, are, 1431.
bees (in the brain), a fantasy, craze, 66.
bee that as bee maie, 1654.
behouff, behoof, advantage, 76.
benefite, that is your, that is to your advantage, 1711.
bent, inclined, resolved, 552.

*****besiraunce,** *for* desirant, desirous, 703.
best(e), best off, most fortunate, 803, 804.
be trust, *past part.,* trusted, 343.
*****bezeivers,** *for* deceivers, 1044.
blisse, to bless, 1348.
bluddinges, black puddings, 851.
blynde, secret, privy, 99.
blynde, to hoodwink, 107.
bones, 228, 613, 829, **cockes bones,** 949; **goddes bones,** 702; *an exclamation.*
booke, the, the Bible, 1706.
boote, no, no good, of no avail, 1894.
border, in everye, within the boundaries, everywhere, 1457.
borne in hand, treated, managed, governed, 969.
borrowe, ransom, save, 597.
botcherie, botching, clumsy or shoddy work, 1742.
bote, boat, 'have an ore in everye bodies b.', 1152.
boulte, to bolt, sift, 'sifte and b.', to examine matters, 589.
bourde, to bourd *is either* to jest *or* to joust: *here prob. confused with, or an error for,* board, to accost, 331, 436.
bourdened, burdened, charged, accused, 1763.
box, thrash, overcome, 313.
boy, *a dog's name,* 313.
breake, break off, interrupt, put an end to, 167, 1228; initiate, 1491.
bridle, to harness up, get going, 1308.
brode, broad, outspoken, vulgar, 743.
broklettes, 96, *possibly* brooklets (*cf.* driblets, 95), *but the form is not recorded before xix cent., the earlier being* brookets: *perh. rather an unrecorded dim. of* brokes, fragments.
brueth, is brewing, is afoot, 1308.
bruted, bruited, spoken of, 78.
brym, breme, loud, prevalent, 1280.
*****bum,** by my, 665, 1158.
bunting, 769, *app. the bird, but prob. assoc. with the part. adj.* bunting,

GLOSSARY

swelling or plump, *recorded slightly later*.
buttons, round knobs, *here app.* fat purses, 771.
bycloked, by cloaked or hidden, 23.
*byd, bided, tarried, 1614.
byde, await, brook, 523.
by drede, ? free from dread, 114 (*for* by = from *see* O.E.D. *sense* 6a).
by hooke or by crooke, 169.

C

cale, call, 1689.
Callis, Calais, 782.
can (thanke), con, offer, give (thanks), 794.
*captyvytee, *for* capacity, ability, understanding, 653.
care, 'I doe care', I am filled with anxiety, 892.
carping, speaking, cavilling, 743.
carrye yn, go in, take cover, 1452.
case, in, provided that, 815.
casualties, casual or incidental payments at law, 99.
cataill, 500, cattall, 666, cattle.
catche, lay hands on, acquire, 174.
*catche awoorde that might catche, get in a word who could, 1587.
catche that catche maye, 172.
catif, caitiff, villain, 432.
caughtst, didst gain or acquire, 1898.
cayes, keys, 119 (*cf.* kye).
certaine, certainly, indeed, 16.
certes, certainly, indeed, 616.
*cha, *see* che.
chafing, fretful, 167.
chaine, 'whipp over the chaine', 1755.
chalenging, claiming fulfilment of, 972.
*cham, *see* che.
champion, champaign, open, level, 446.
charge, office, 329.
*chave, *see* che.
chaunge, exchange, 796.
*chawas, *see* che.
*che, *shortened form of* iche, I, 639, 1812; *common in compounds*, cha, I have, 689, 696, 1090, 1820;

chad, I had, 1021, 1023, 1025, 1077, 1104; cham, I am, 1022, 1128, 1622; chave, I have, 1600; chawas (? *error for* chwas *or* che was), I was, 1082; chil(l), I will, 641, 717, 721, 726, 736, 1140, 1580; choulde, I should, *or* I would, 1000, 1026, 1578, 1589, 1611, 1614; chwas, I was, 703, 1026, 1586 (*cf.* erche, shalche).
checking, reproof, 1542.
chiefe ... of price, most eminent, foremost, 1375.
*chil(l), *see* che.
*childe, fellow (*contemptuous*), 682.
childe, 'with child to heare', desirous of hearing, 236.
childes parte, inheritance, share, 178.
chive, achieve, 140.
chone, *see* every chone.
choppe, bargain, 801; thrust, 923.
*choulde, *see* che.
christendome, christianity, 358.
*chwas, *see* che.
clawbacke, flatterer, 183.
clawe, 'c.st...myne elbowe', 182, 'c. hir elbowe', 269. To claw by the sleeve *is* to flatter (O.E.D., claw, v. sense 4): *here the primary idea seems to be rather* to pluck at the sleeve (*to attract attention*), *but that of flattery runs through* 183–6.
cleane, 271, clene, 155, wholly, altogether.
clogg, impediment, hindrance, 1559.
clowterie, clouting, clumsy or shoddy work, 1742 (*cf.* botcherie).
clowtes, clouts, rags, 870.
*cobbes, great men, lords, 1095.
cockes, *perversion of* God's, 949, 1867.
cognisaunce, emblem, device, 'impresa', 1792.
coigne, coin, coinage, 1074, 1624.
*coilled, beaten, 1811.
collusion, secret agreement, fraud, 23.
*come owt, become known, 699.
*commediens, *for* commodious *and* convenient, 669.
commodius, profitable, convenient, 73.

GLOSSARY

commontie, commonality, *Dram. Pers.*
communication, conversation, manner of speech, 208.
comoditie, -ee, commodity, convenience, interest, advantage, profit, 526, 1007, 1133, 1809; belongings, property, 632.
comons, 1358, *might of course be either* common lands *or* common people, *but perh. rather* common funds, state revenue.
co(u)mpace, *sb.*, compass, plan, device, 1033, 1035; 'the compace to fetch', the plan to devise, 67; 'vet to ferre a coumpace abowte', to proceed too indirectly, 1016.
co(u)mpace, *vb.*, to compass, plan, devise, bring about, 1015, 1035; **coumpaced,** 1032, 1033; **coumpacing,** *vb. sb.*, 1031 (2), 1032, 1043.
compacte, *part part.*, consolidated, 1545.
compares, compeers, companions, 1505.
complices, associates, *perh.* accomplices, 1515.
*****comporte (Iscomporte),** ? *for* report, refer, appeal, 1030.
conceipte, conceit, mental condition, frame of mind, 905.
condinge, condign, fitting, 628.
contribution, wrong, extortion, 1898.
conveighe, convey, take, 1054.
conveighed, conveyed, removed, 1521.
converte, turn, 1214.
convinced, convicted, 1381.
conynger, more cunning, 1839.
cooste, coast, part, 152.
*****copped,** saucy, proud, 692.
coppie, example, 'chaunge our c.', alter our behaviour, 475.
corda, *see* trussing corda.
corne fedde, wilbe, will have of the best, 316.
corners, ? secret devices, 965.
corrupte, (*with sense of earlier* corrumpte) spoil, mar (*or* ? *for* correct, punish), 694; **corroupt,** *past part.* spoiled, destroyed, 1592.

coumpace, *see* compace.
counterfai(c)te, counterfeit, 418, 419, 429.
*****courtnalls,** court-nolls, *a contemptuous term for* courtiers (*common in would-be dialect*), 1585.
covent, convent, monastery, 884.
covetise, covetouisness, 80, 352, &c.
covetous, (*by confusion for*) covetise, 260 (2).
crekes, creeks, tricks, artifices, 878.
crow, to cry out (insolently), 1146.
crowe, 'the c. is white', 'the swanne is blacke', *expression of what we should call* yes-men, 184.
crummes, scraps, trifles, 1850.
*****custoditee,** *for* custody, 1808.
custome, rent, duty, 873.
cutte my throte, *interj.*, 232.

D

daisie, to leape at a, ? to lie under the sod, to turn up one's toes, 1322.
dawe, (jackdaw) simpleton, 1145; **dawes,** 879, 1112.
dearling, darling, 1922; **derling mooste dere,** 1202, 1814.
debtor, 'I am a debtor', I am bound, 1013.
decayed, impaired, impoverished, 484.
declaracion, explanation, the clearing up of a matter, 1045.
dedicate, dedicated, 5.
*****defende, godde,** God forbid, 708.
delated, dilated, expanded, uplifted, 1231.
depe (heads), profound, subtle, 620.
derling, *see* dearling.
descryed, seen for what it is, exposed, 1722.
desolacion, devastation, destruction, 577.
desperablie, *adv.*, despairably (*only the adj. is recorded*), 1230 (*the spelling perh. influenced by* desperately).
*****destructions,** *for* instructions, 1142, 1143.
detected, accused, 84.
determinacyon, 379, *prob.* decision

GLOSSARY

(*the sense of* definition *appears to be later*).
devises, purposes, intentions, 1873.
devyll ys a knave, the, 174.
directe, directed, sent, 1924.
directrie, directory, *adj.*, directive (*or poss. sb.* guide, *but in early use more usually a book or index*), 1795.
*****diuum este, iusllum weste,** *for* diuites estis iuste fuistes (*Brandl*), 1090.
doo you tunderstaunde, give you to understand, 1455.
double, doubly, 551, 553, 1346.
doulfull, doleful, 201.
dragged vp, dredged, netted, 1758.
drouping, drooping, despondent, 605.
dureth, endures, lasts, 1181.
dyete, diet, 'are not for oure d.', do not suit our way of life, 1464.

E

eagrenesse, sharpness, vindictiveness, 1173.
eare, e'er, ever, 1051.
eastate, *see* estate.
eche where, everywhere, 363.
echone, each one, 63.
Edwardes, coins (*of various values*), 767.
*****eft whiles,** again, 987 (*app. not recorded, but formed on anal. of* eft-sithes).
*****either other,** each other, 987.
elated, raised, 1232.
elbowe, 'e. rowme', elbow room, a standing, 258; 'pranketh she hir e.se', *see under* side.
elfe, imp, a mischievous person, 259, 1831; **elfes,** 1011.
emend(e), *vb.*, amend, 705, 707.
emendement, amendment, 970.
emendes, *sb.*, amends, reparation, 1173.
emong(e), among, 124, 167, 363, 575; **emonges,** 273, 778.
emongst, amongst, 1440, 1821.
emprowed, improved, *partic.* (land) enclosed, 809.

enbrace, embrace, 1351, 1353.
encroached, seized, 856.
encrochinge, seizure, 293.
ende, 'be ever att one e.', always form part (of what you say), 270.
endyte, indict, arraign, 1522.
enfourmed, fashioned, 805.
*****enquest,** *for* request, 1128.
*****envies,** *for* enviers, ill-wishers, *or perh. for* enemies (*see* O.E.D., Envy, *sb.* ¶), 1612.
er, e'er, ever, 883, 1414.
er, ere, before, 1269.
*****erche,** ere che, before I, 1163.
ery, e'ery, every, 1328.
establishment, establishing, settlement, 1388.
e(a)state, rank, condition, 237, 1411, 1496, 1922; **eastates,** 1790.
esteme, esteem, judge, believe, 1361.
ever still, 28 (*cf.* evermore).
every(e) chone, everych one, everyone, 59, 819, &c.
*****evill,** ill, misfortune, 1813.
*****exaltacions,** *for* exhortations, advice, 1140.
excheates, escheats, forfeitures, levies, plunder, 99.
Ex ore infantium perfecisti laudem, 41, *see* Psal. viii. 3 (A.V. viii. 2), Matt. xxi. 16.
extente, valuation, assessment, 810.
extraictes, 100, *unrecorded, but app. a var. of* extracts, *occasionally used for* extreats, estreats: 'scape of e.', ? a payment to avoid estreat.

F

*****face,** to brave, bully, 701.
facing owt, out-facing, browbeating, 879.
facion, fashion, 521.
factes, crimes, 86.
failles, withowte all, without fail, without any doubt, 165 (*the pl. is for the sake of the rhyme*).
faire, *adj.*, mere, sheer, 155.
faire, *adv.*, civilly, kindly, 941.
fall, an overthrow (*in wrestling*), 467.
fall, fallen, 1542.

GLOSSARY

fall back fall edge, whatever happens, 1467 (O.E.D. *not bef.* 1622, *but in* Lindsay's *Satire of the Three Estates*).
fansie, 'I iudge in my f.', I imagine, 835.
fansie, for your, to satisfy your whim, 1727.
favors, good will, 199.
feate, action, purpose, 79.
feather, 'f. my neste', 88, 'f. oure nestes', 915, 'f. well his neaste', 1846; 'geve a fether for agoose', make a good bargain, 796.
ferme, a farm, 798.
ferme (of), to farm out (to), 960 (*but of may be a miswriting*).
ferre, far, 603, 625, 1010, 1016, 1793.
ferther, *adv.*, further, 1315.
ferther, *vb.*, further, advantage, advance, 1883.
*****ferthest, at the**, at the end of my journey, 986.
festinacion, haste, 524.
fetch a compace, *see under* compace.
fether, *see* feather.
fett(e), fetch, 515, 517, 522, 1802.
*****fichaunte**, ? fitchant (O.E.D. *first in* 1600), nimble, 1821.
first or laste, early or late, 1348 (O.E.D. *not bef.* 1700, 'sooner or later').
*****fisike**, to physic, dose, treat, 987.
flaterabundus (*nonce form. after Lat., cf.* 461), full of flattery, 183. *Cf.* populorum.
fliereth on youe, mocks you, 680; *cf.* flyering, fleering, mocking, 183.
fliettance, 97, *unrecorded, but* ? fleetance (*from* fleet, to float), things carried on the surface of a stream, driftwood.
flixe, flux, running, dysentery, 1907.
florent, flourishing, 441.
flyce, fleece, share of booty (*sense transferred from vb.*), 174; **flycynges**, 102.
flyced, fleeced, ? flayed, 820.
flyering, *see under* fliereth.
flyghth, flieth, 1294.
flytched, sliced, 792.
foorthwarde, forward, 337 S.D.

foorth with all, immediately, 338.
for, ? in accordance with (*but perh. repeated from prev. line by mistake for* by), 585; 'f. me', so far as I am concerned, 699, 1644; 'rydde f. me', rid of me (*but perh. a miswriting*), 1504; 'f. wo', to the point of hurting, 770; **forre**, 1936.
force, no, no matter, 1555.
fore pondred, considered beforehand, prepared, 9.
forfayctes, forfeits, fines, 100.
forthe taken, advanced, put in a position of authority, 492 (O.E.D. *quotes* Palsgrave, 1530, 'I take forthe a man, I avance hym'). *Cf.* sett yow foorth.
*****for yet**, forgotten, 696.
fownder, founder, one who supports or maintains (O.E.D., *sense* 4), leader, 150, 173, 203, 227, 319, 322, 323, 340, 342; **founder**, 256; **foundre**, 265; 'founder me no foundring', 204.
fraie, I, I am afraid, 475.
frame, to 'turn out', 821; to prosper, 1331.
framynge, fashioning, 1541.
frendelier, *adv.*, friendlier, in a more salutary manner, 1134.
frewte, 731, **fruicte**, 1532, fruit.
fume, anger, 206.
furres, thieves (*from L.* fur), 286.
fyfte, fifth, 800 (*but* fifth, 860).

G

gawdes, objects of mockery, sport, 1651.
gawdies, gauds, tricks, pranks, 1754 (*no exact parallel, but* Skelton *has adj.* gaudy *in a similar sense*).
geare, matter, business, 289, 812, 1571, &c.
geate, get, 847, 1024, 1676, 1896.
generall, common, not particular, 1291.
*****gentman**, gentleman, 1067. *Cf.* ientman.
geve, give, *passim* (*but* give, 956); 'g. a fether for agooce', make a good bargain, 796.
ghostelye, spiritual, *but here* g. pur-

GLOSSARY

pose *simply* what is in your mind, 215.
*gisse, *perversion of* Jesus, 1165. *Cf.* Iisse.
gobbet, piece, portion, 795.
goddamighties, God-Almighties, bags of money, 951.
goddiggod, God give you good (day), 59, 60, 61, 63; goddigod eve, goddigod spede, 1636.
*godsgood, of, ownerless, worthless (O.E.D.), 1028.
goe, a, *see* agoe.
gooce, 'geve a fether for ag.', make a good bargain, 796.
good(e), wealth, 996; 'in g. houre be ytt spoken', absit omen, 117; 'of g. love', out of kindness, with good intent, 190; 'g. night', farewell to, 1694.
goodnes, good, 'abought litle g.', 1618.
goodspede, *perh. for* God-speed, *see under* waye.
gosse, by, by God, 315 (gos *properly for* God's, *as in* gos bones, *but here some noun is understood*).
gotten, *past part.*, got, 1761.
*got vp, scraped together, 1077.
goverment, government, 1816.
grace, gift, 1439, 'a faire g.', mere good fortune, a piece of luck, 155; 'a tyme of g.', a propitious moment, 436.
grasse, 'or anie g. maie growe on hir hele', 946; 'while the g. shall growe the horse shall sterve', 1120.
greace, grace, 547.
greate waie hens, a, far and wide, 386.
grene che(e)se, 'made youe beeleve the moone was a g. c.', 1779; 'ye can see no g. c. but your teeth wyll watier', 762.
grosse, plain, evident, 1283.
grosseree, 1745 (*might be* grossing, engrossing, 'cornering', *but in the context prob. merely*) grossness, ill behaviour.
grote, groat, trifling sum, 1691.
*grotte, groat, 'cannot bestowe their g.', can get nothing for their pennies, 1098.

grownde, place, spot, 828; land, 1020.
grum(b)le sede, gromwell seed, money, 82, 465.
grunte, grumble, 1155; grunted, 211.
grutche, *sb.*, complaint, resentment, 214, &c.; *vb.*, complain, 799.
gubbins, gobbets, fragments, parings, 98.
gyptian, 1194, *see p. xxi.*

H

ha, have, 647, 1017, 1561, 1562, 1808, &c.
*hable, able, strong, 1026; 'iche am h. to', I can, 1599.
haie, haye, hey ('used in the burden of a song with no definite meaning', O.E.D.), 1661.
hake, *an exclamation perh. imitative of clearing the throat*, 247, 825.
hale, hall, 1695.
*haled vp, brought up, educated, 1820.
halfe, 'on goddes h.', in God's name, 776.
halowes, saints, 203.
hamper, restrain, 574.
handes under the side, *see under* side.
hanging stuff, make good, be fit for the gallows, 376.
happe, *sb.*, fortune, 469, 994; 'happie happe', lucky chance, 1059.
happe, *vb.*, to happen to, 1322.
harde, hard, 1585, 1748.
harde, heard, 368, 476, 689, 1011, 1051, 1090, 1201, 1222, 1367 (hard), 1490.
hardelie, hardily, steadily, 'h. stand there styll', be sure not to move, 853.
hare, *see under* thieke.
harmes, come to his, come to harm, 831.
haste, in, quickly, at once, 1734.
*hate, ha'it, have it, 1080.
haulfe, half, 781, 1827.
have after, to follow, 950.
have an ore in everye bodies bote, have a finger in every pie, 1152.

74   GLOSSARY

have att, *see under* petticote.
have on the lips, be struck in the mouth, 415.
have ye, may ye have, 634.
heade, on, ahead, 362.
headie, headstrong, 1797.
heale, health, 636, 1890.
heare, here, 177, 306, 613, &c.; heareabowt, 162.
heare, her, 941.
heare, hair, 927, 928; 'a heare', in the least, 1650; *'make volkes h. growe throughe their hood', *see under* make.
hedge, *see under* youe will over the hedge.
*hele, he'll, he will, 689.
hem, to make a hemming noise, 828.
hens, hence, 368, 580, 1010, 1160, 1559, 1561.
her, here, 1316.
here, hear, 1317.
hey making, profitable activity, 901.
hidden, being concealed, 24.
Hieresalem (*perh. miswriting for* Hierusalem), Jerusalem, 42.
hir, her, 108, 109, &c. (*but* her, 107).
holsome, wholesome, 528, 1420.
holydome, halidom, relic; 'by my h.', *a common asseveration*, 357, 1104, 1256.
holye gooste, inspired intelligence (*ironical*), 151.
homelye, rough, 792.
honestie, reputation, good name, 361.
honores mutant mores . . . raro in meliores, 1509–10.
hoo, *interj.*, stop; 'saie h.', cry 'enough', 300.
hood, 'make . . . volkes heare growe throughe their h.', *see under* make.
hooe, who, 481.
hooke, 'by h. or by crooke', 169.
hoorde, to hoard, 844.
hornes, to pluck in his, *as a snail its feelers*, 1523.
horse, 'while the grasse shall growe the h. shall sterve', 1120.
hotte, fresh, recent, 1280.
hough, *interj.*, ho, hey, 898 S.D.

hourded, hoarded, 1762.
how, *interj.*, ho, 1615.
*howrecop, horecop, bastard, 679, 697, 715, 1593.
hucking, haggling, bargaining, traffic, endeavour, 1676.
hundreth, hundred, 226; hunderd, 791, 955; *but* hundred, 1434.
hyppe, hip; 'have you on the h.', have you at advantage (*a wrestling term*), 742.

I J

*I, in, 1016.
*I- (*of past part.*), I bee, I pilate, I polde, I pounst, I strike, I torment, I trounst: *see the simple forms*.
iacke, fellow, knave, 180.
iacke a napes, a monkey, 1755.
iangling, babbling, prating, 947, 1107.
iapes, tricks, devices, 1754.
iavels, rascals, 264.
*iche, I, 641, 710, 999, 1040, 1590, 1592, 1777; itche, 648; yche, 1039; *in combination*, I cham, I am, 986; I chil(l), ichill, I will, 739, 1606, 1830; ichwin, I ween, 1084. *Cf.* is.
ielousie, mistrust, suspicion, 86. *Cf.* zelousye.
ientilman, gentleman (*ironic*), 1623.
ientle, gentle, 939.
*ientman, gentleman, 1006, 1031. *Cf.* gentman.
*ieoperde, to risk, 1606; *see also under* ioinct.
*ignoram, *for* ignorant, 648, 665; *so* ignorams, ignorant folk, 992.
*Iisse, *perversion of* Jesus, 1092, 1807. *Cf.* gisse.
in (my consciens), on, 369; (the vertue of God), by, 1756 (*perh. by analogy with* in the name of God).
in and owte, inside out, 420.
in continent, immediately, 1359.
informacions, instruction, 1139.
in good houre be ytt spoken, absit omen, 117.
interesse, profit, interest, 857.
iobbes, lumps, packages, 881.

GLOSSARY

Iohn, 'I. holde my stafe', 'what is the clocke', *a hanger-on prepared for any service*, 185.
Iohn lacke latten, *an unlearned clerk*, 959.
ioigning, joining, 719.
ioincte, 'ieoperde a i.', 1606; 'tadventure a i.', 1468; to risk a limb.
*Is, I (*always in combination with the following word, which is glossed if necessary*): Iscan, 677, 1024, 1050; Iscannot, 684, 991, 1821; Iscomporte, 1030; iscrye, 718; Isdare, 1578; Isfearde, 1590; isfynde, 717; Isner, I never, 1777; Ispraie, 1011; Isrecke, 1088; Isshoulde, 1592; Isthanke, 1600; Isvele, I feel, 1020.
*itche, *see* iche.
Iusticia tamen non luxit in nobis... tourned into wormwoode, 1530–2, *cf.* Amos, v. 7, 'Qui conuertitis in absinthium iudicium, et iusticiam in terra relinquitis'.
I wis, certainly, 1541, 1601, 1767; I wisse, 1539.
Iyll, Gill, 'I. myne owne mare', 1560 (O.E.D. *quotes* Gill *as a mare's name c.* 1650; *perh. from Sc.* gillot, a mare). *Cf.* ryde.

K

*ka, quoth a, 1031, 1043.
*kine, cows, 1021.
kye, key, 156. *Cf.* cayes.
*kyxe, kex, a dry stalk, 1906.

L

lacke, to spare, do without, 103; 'l. who l. shall', 316.
*ladidome, ladyship, 703.
laie on lode, lay the load on, do your carting, 900.
laisure, opportunity, 736.
lammas, the first of August, harvest-home; 'latter l.', the Greek calends, never, 813.
learning, information, 848.
leat(e), leatte, to let, 56, 235, 322, &c.

lese, to lose, 106.
lest, least, 359.
lett, to hinder, 189, 516.
lewde, common, unseemly, 212.
lightlye, at once, 1900.
likelihood, of, in all probability, 1242.
livelood, livelihood, 924, 1847.
lo(e), to look, 1165, 1219 (*the imper. of this verb passes insensibly into the interj.*).
lode, load, *see* laie on lode.
lone, a, alone, unique, 82.
longtong, babbler, 1705; long-tounged, blabbing, 910.
looce, loose, 1841; free, unappropriated, 795.
looke, expect, 124; search for, 1265.
looke after, look for, seek, 161.
looke for, expect, 1329.
losel, ne'er-do-well, 1620.
lotte, portion, 320, 1904.
lowtes, fools, 'of their plate... we made them l.', we fooled them out of their plate, 869.
loytring, idle, vagabond, 1620.
luste, to list, wish, desire, 346, 495, 774, 780, 1505, 1628.
lustye, pleasant, unrestricted, 310.
lye, 'let me l.', may I be lying, *or rather* I shall fail of my purpose, 258.
lyve daies, life-days, 120.
*lyver, deliver, 1910 (*the form is common*).
lyvinges, possessions, 282.

M

mace, *see* mass.
*madge mason, *for* imagination, 655.
*make, make up, collect, 1078; 'm.... volkes heare [hair] growe throughe their hood', make them wear tattered clothes, reduce to poverty, 1036.
make bate, discord maker, 1703.
make vp my mouth, to furnish my meal with a special dainty, to collect tit-bits, 88.
malkin, 644, *familiar dimin. of* Matilda *or* Maud, *used generically*

for a woman; 'malkin ist', this is she.
mallis, malice, 1719.
manier, manner, *passim*.
manier, maniour, stolen property, 'with the m.', with the goods, in the act, 1763.
manne, servant, 739.
markett, business, affairs, 591.
marye masse, a mass in honour of the Virgin, 471, 1855.
masse, mas, master, 1025; **mace,** 1006.
masse, by the mass, 303. *Cf.* marye masse.
masship, mastership, 813, 841, 1053.
matier, matter, 4, 216, 222, 223, 761, &c.; **mattier,** 39; **mattiers,** 745.
measure, to measure out, apportion, 282.
mell, to meddle, interfere, 692, 1150, 1466.
*****member,** *for* remember, 684; ponder, 1142.
*****mende,** 'zo god me m.', *a mere asseveration*, 1580.
meneth, meaneth, speaketh, 54.
merchaunte, fellow, 182; **merchauntes,** 1848.
mervaile, a marvel, 457.
*****messe,** a company of four, 677.
misconstred, misconstrued, 10.
miser, wretch, 1143.
Misericordia et veritas sibi obuiauerunt, 1284, *see* Psal. lxxxiv. 11 (A.V. lxxxv. 10).
mo(o), more, 103, 105, 512, &c., 'm. then he', besides him, 582.
mome, dolt, 348.
mone, moan, lament, 1621.
mone, moon, 758.
money sweeter then sugar, 287–8.
monishe, admonish, warn, 1571, 1615.
moon, *see under* grene chese.
mooste, utmost, 135.
moothed, mouthed, 1535.
mot, *vb.*, mote, may; *'so m. I thee', 715; **mowte,** 'so m. I goe', 138; *mere asseverations*.
mote, a speck of dust, 564.
mouth, *see under* make.

mowght, might, 244.
mowte, *misspelling of* mote, *see* mot.
mued, ? mewed, shed, *or perh. error for* mown, 902 (mew *is a xvi-cent. spelling of* mow, to grimace, *but is not recorded for* mow, to cut grass; *moreover the past part. of the latter is always strong*).
*****mustres,** mistress, 645.
myserie, miserliness, 1743.
mysters, masters, governors, 598 (*but perh. a miswriting*: O.E.D. *has only one quot. for* mister (1551) *before the xviii cent.*).

N

naked, ? unprotected, 1303.
*****nam** (not), ne am, am not, 1823.
naughtie, nawghtie, evil, wicked, 582, 1799, 1831.
ner(e), ne'er, never, 190, 537, 1014, 1294, 1672, &c.
nere, near, 1393; nearer, 710 (**neare**), 1317, 1820; *doubtful,* 543, 776, 886, 1819 (**ner**).
niene, nine, 846 (*but* nyne, 845).
*****nil,** ne will, will not, 1087, 1820; **nil not,** 692; **nylnot,** 693.
*****ninnat, nynnat,** will not, 1604, 1822.
*****nold,** ne wold, would not, 1817.
nominacion, name, designation, 428.
nonce, 'for the n.', for the occasion, intent on the moment, in a hurry, 232; **nones,** 'for the n.', immediately, 517.
none, not any, no, 970.
not where, not anywhere, nowhere, 1633 (*but* not *may be a miswriting for* no).
nowe of daies, now-a-days, 1431.
nowe to thee, now it is your turn, 1892.
*****nylnot,** *see under* nil.
nymphes, maidens, attendants, 1483.

O

occasion, opportunity, 1856.
od ends, remnants, fragments left over, odds and ends, 95.

GLOSSARY

of, by, 758, 1244; out of, from, 189, 190, 554, 1886.
of, off, 491, 666, 1752, 1754, 1773, &c.; 'looke o. from', look away from, take your eyes off, 761.
*om, 'em, them, 677, 694, 1050, 1604, 1608, 1609, 1613, 1777, 1805.
on bowne viage, un bon voyage, 597.
one, 'as well as one', as well as any-one, 176.
ones, once, 284, 518, 1835 (*but* once, 231). *Cf.* ons.
on heade, ahead, 362.
*ons, one's, 1604.
ons, once, 460, 509, 1228, 1395, 1888; already, now, 1467, 1478, 1517, 1641.
*ont, on't, of it, 1084.
open, that thing, disclose that matter, 277.
open mowthed, clamorous, blabbing, 1051.
or, ere, before, 1767; 'or anie grasse maie growe on hir hele', with all speed, 946.
ore, oar, 1152; *and see under* have.
orels, or else (*usually one word*), 304, *and passim.*
organes, musical (wind) instruments; 'plaieth at o.', fingers (as if playing on an instrument), 1246.
other, others, 1043.
oughe, owe, 274.
ought, out, 1904.
owte, *interj.*, out (*an exclamation of surprise or indignation*), 1756.

P

*paile, 1021, *either* pale, fence, enclosure; *or* pail, 'to my p.', for milking.
painfull, painstaking, diligent, 1129.
pardee, *lit.* by God; verily, 1166, 1300.
pardon, leave, permission, 1900.
pashe (of god), passion, 1645, 1907; passhen, 785 (*but* passion, 229, 1867).
passe, *sb.*, issue, end, 1854.

passe, *vb.*, to have care; 'on myne honestie p.', consider my good name, 361.
*passeive, *for* perceive, 666.
paste, gone, lost, 1632.
patcherie, the behaviour of a patch or fool, knavery, 1740.
paules steeple, the steeple of St. Paul's, 635; *polle steple, 1010.
peaching, informing, 1837.
*peake, peek, peep, look, 1582.
*peason, *for* peasant, 701.
penie dole, by, in driblets, 866.
perfeicte, perfect, 1889; perfitte, 279; perfytte, 1396.
*perke, to thrust oneself forward, 1823.
*permounted, ? *for* promoted, advanced, encouraged, 1598.
permutacions, bartering, exchange, 807.
persans, Persians, 447.
*perswaged, *for* persuaded, 1128.
perswasion, argument, argufying, 926.
*pertelye, pertly, apertly, openly, briskly, 1026.
*perzente, *for* represent, 648.
pestell, 409; pestle, 1288; pestilence, plague.
petie, petty, minor, 102.
petticote, waistcoat, under-coat, 1892; 'have att thye p.', with the idea of stripping.
pieke, pick, 1570; 'p. me home', ? pick my way home, 1591.
piekpurse, pickpurse, 1246, 1248, 1250; piekepurses, 1767.
pielouries, pillories, 1249.
Piers Piekpurse, 1246, 1250.
*pilate (I pilate), *past part.* Pilated, brought before Pilate, 650.
pipes, ? bags, purses, 472.
pippe, *a disease (properly of fowls)*, 741.
pitcheree (*unrecorded*), 1640, 'begging with a pitcher (a northern custom)'—Magnus.
place, in right, at the right moment, 1162.
place of the strete, no, nowhere in the street, 1433.

78   GLOSSARY

plaie, activity, business, 1150.
*plaine me, complain, 1040.
pleasaunce, of, for pleasure, 1625.
please, an, if it please, 557.
*plentye, plentiful, 721.
plounge, plunge, stress, strait, disaster, 1572, 1902.
plucke, sb., snatch, pillage, 816.
poincte, a point, tag, lace, trifle, 1605.
poincte, at a, come to the point, ready, resolved, 1467.
poke, sack, 1843.
*polde (I polde), past part., shorn, fleeced, plundered, 649. Cf. polle.
*policate, for politic (? with a suggestion of polecat), 697.
polle, shear, plunder, rob, 843.
*polle steple, see paules steeple.
poore, to pour, 1734.
*popt, popped, put, 1594.
populorum, 'by his precious p.', an oath or expletive in which a humorous nonce-formation of no precise meaning has been substituted for the effective word, 1649. Cf. flaterabundus.
porte, style of living, 310.
*pounst (I pounst), past part., bruised, 650 (var. of punched).
poure, power, 255, 1408.
powre, to pour, 1736.
practise, proceedings, perh. machinations, trickery, 1786.
praies, sb., preys, 98.
pranketh, see under side.
preast, prest(e), ready, eager, 548, 1479, 1710.
*premydence, for pre-eminence, 686.
price, prize, share, 326; worth, estimation, 'chiefe . . . of p.', most eminent, foremost, 1375.
prioure of Prickingham, 884.
progresse, to go on progress, travel, 1457.
progression, advancement, 220.
prosecuted, put into effect, 1860.
*proute, prowte, proud, 1593; glad, 1598.
provestes, provosts, presidents of the chapter, 1848.
prying, peeping in, 1577.

putte, to posit, entertain, allow, 608.
pynne, ? pitch, note; 'sett on a merrie p.', 594 (the phrase is proverbial and perh. derived from tuning a stringed instrument by turning a pin or peg).

Q

quaisie, queasy, unsettled, ticklish, 1321.
qualified, appeased, 940.
quite, wholly, entirely, 1521.

R

rahated, rated, reproved, 364.
rake, rake in, gather, 82, 176.
rather, earlier, 197.
raught, reached, 1548.
raweclothes, raw or unfulled cloth, 876.
reade, advice, 1159.
*reade, to guess, tell, 676.
reast, rest, what is over, 796.
recke not, care not, do not object, 889, (Isrecke) 1088.
recover, to set right, remedy, cure, 460, 599, 1200, 1859.
recure, restore, 1406; recured, cured, amended, 1415.
redowne, redound, contribute, 570, 1133.
redresse, sb., remedy, 466, 1860, 1927; amendment, 981.
redresse, vb., remedy, 1862.
refused, shunned, 1370.
regarde, to have in regard, value, 558.
relacion, report, 1002.
renne, to run, 1659; renne, past part., run, 1000; renneth, 905; rennyng, 1631.
repeale, to reform, amend, 1786.
replenished, stocked or filled, 1190.
repyneth, murmurs, complains, 823.
restorytee, a restorative, 888.
rewine, ruin, 599.
rewle, sb., rule, order, government, 22, 334, &c.
rewle, vb., rule, 140, 521, &c.; 'r. (*roile) all the roste', 136, 689.

GLOSSARY

*Rice puddingcake, *for* Respublica, 636, 637, 1007, (*one word*) 1612.
rigg, *a dog's name*, 340.
*roile, rule (*see* rewle, *vb.*); roilled, roylled, rolde, ruled 693, 1810, 1817.
rome, room, place, 789.
ronne on heade, run ahead (inconsiderately), 362.
roode, a cross, 493, throod, 1035.
roste, roast, *see under* rewle.
rowme (elbowe r.), room, space, 258.
rumbeling, making a tumult, 263.
ryde vppon Iyll myne owne mare, look after my own interests, 1506.

S

saieth (youe), say, 1878.
Saincte George the borowe, Saint George save thee, 597.
Saincte Tronnion, the Holy Trinity, 1694 (O.E.D., Trunnion, *? perversion of Tri(n)-union*; 1577 *Misogonus*, iv. ii, Gods trunnion).
*sallet, salade, helmet, 1027.
salve festa dies, Ovid, *Fasti*, i. 87, 1499.
scambling, *see* skamble.
scape, escape, *see under* extraictes.
scraped, scraped together, collected, 1850; scrapedst vp, 1896.
scudde, hastened, 1632.
*season, period of time, while, 1017.
sectourship(p), secutorship, executorship, 863, 865.
seens, *see* sens.
see place, bishop's palace, 804.
selie, simple, 941.
sens, since, 764, 936, 1817; seeing that, 1565; already, 260, 319 (syns), 532 (seens), 763 (syens), 1599, 1730.
sente, *earlier and better spelling of* scent, 164.
sett, sat, 764; 's. on a merie pynne', *see under* pynne; 's. yowe foorth', advanced you, 838; 's. youe yn', *?* to set you on the way, 147 (*perh. connected with the phrase* 'to set in foot', to enter upon an undertaking).
*shaked, shook, 1586.

*shalche, shall che, shall I, 1609, 1920.
*shales, shells, husks, 725 (*distinct from* shells *though ultimately related*).
shall, must, 234; will, 1120, 1127.
sharinges, what is cut off, shearings, 94.
shente, blamed, 14.
shrewe, to beshrew, curse, 1303.
shriddinges, shreddings, prunings, trimmings, 102.
shuttle, *var. of* shittle, unsteady, 1293.
shwere, swear, 1649 (*perh. a miswriting, though recorded as a xvicent. spelling*).
shwete, 1866; shewete, 108 (*perh. miswritings of* swete, *as at* 231; *but cf.* shwere).
side, 'looke a lofte with handes vnder the s.', 276; 'than pranketh she hir elbowse owte vnder hir s.', 1796. (*The sense is obscure; but the idea seems to be that of striking a combative or arrogant attitude. To prank, is to caper or prance, 'esp. with suggestion of display or arrogance'*, *perh.* to strut, parade, *and also to dress, deck, in a showy manner*.)
sigthes, sighs, 1213.
sindons, fine linen cloths, corporals, 872.
sitt but in small reste, *see under* small reste.
skamble, *earlier form of* scramble, struggle voraciously, 176; skambling (sc-), 318, 868.
skeymishe, squeamish, backward, 278.
*skitbrained, harebrained, 1811; skitbraines, 1817 (*prob. associated with* skittish).
slabbe, to gobble, 852.
slacke, *adj.* slack, behindhand, 1646.
slake, to abate, mitigate, 1416.
sluttish, dirty, 853.
slypper, slippery, deceitful, 679.
smale reste, 'sytt but in s. r.', have little ease 304 (*perh. with reference to the stocks*).

GLOSSARY

smelled a ratte, had our suspicions aroused, 162.
*smoult, smolt, affable, 715.
*snatche, a grab, blow, 1588.
snuffeth, snuffs, snorts, 1460; snuffing, 774.
softe, adv. 'as an exclamation with imperative force, either to enjoin silence (825) or deprecate haste (261 (2), 542, 1289)', O.E.D.
solfe, to sing sol-fa, 410.
somes, some people's, 1730.
sore, an ill thing, 116.
sormounte, surmount, exceed, 625.
sors, sores, ills, 982.
sorte, company, crew, gang, 1799; *zorte, 1585.
so so, moderately well, 646.
sowte, sought, 1188.
space, duration of time, 'in this s.', meanwhile, 783.
spaignell, spaniel, 340.
spedde, 'I wilbe s.', I will prosper, 315.
spiede, speedy, 550.
spill, to destroy, 1859.
spittle, hospital, lazar-house, 1848; 's. ladye', a woman thence, 1702.
spoiled, dispoiled, stripped, plundered, 1915, 1923.
*spose, ? for dispute, 1067.
*sqwatte, squash, smash, dash, 1604.
staigh, stay, support, 457.
staighe, stay, state, condition, 735 (a different word).
stalking, stealthy walking, creeping, 160.
standith with more skyll, implies greater ability, 1858.
staring, glaring, looking wildly, 774.
starke, sheer, very, 1112.
state, estate, condition, 1002.
*states, ellip. for men of estate, nobles, 1820 (a use recorded only of estate).
stele, steel, 'as . . . true as s.', 1493.
stelthe, by, in an underhand way, 1003.
stern, rudder, helm, 278.
*sterve, starve, 1120.
stile, see under youe will over the hedge.

stockes, 'syt in niene s.', ? sit nine times in the stocks, 846.
store, 's. (thei saie) is no sore', possessions are no bad thing, 116.
strawes, 'picke s.', gather trifles, 314.
streight, strait, strict, 1862.
*strike (i strike), past part., struck, 1081.
strive, 's. againste the streame', 1443.
*strussioners, 1778, for destructioners acc. to O.E.D., but the context supports Magnus's suggestion of constructioners, people who put (false) constructions or interpretations on things, illusionists, deceivers.
*studd(e), study, employ, 1006; take pains, 1011.
stud(d)ie, take pains, 1012, 1013.
stumbling, falling into error, 934.
sturdie, obstinate, 940.
suche an other, for, for being such, 864.
sufferaunce, allowance, permission, 1769.
summes, totals, 1851.
supersideas, supersedeas, a writ to stay proceedings, 1696.
suspecte, past tense, suspected, 1771.
swanne, see under crow.
swerve, go astray, transgress, 1886.
swette, past part., swetted, 120.
swymmed, swam, glided, 1295.
syens, syns, see sens.

T

tainter hookes, tenter-hooks, 1550.
take, taken, caught, 1612, 1763.
take, to, (allow me) to take, 564.
take hym vp, rebuke him, 934.
take vppon me, assert myself, assume authority, 292; 'tooke muche vppon theim', behaved arrogantly, 1073.
*tall, tale, 663 (perh. a miswriting, but the spelling is recorded).
tarie laisure, tarry leisure, await opportunity, 736.

GLOSSARY

teeth(e) . . . wat(i)er, 762, 1730, *older form of the expression* mouth water, *but not before* 1600, O.E.D.
tenne bones, fingers, 1853.
teverye, to every, 1904.
than, then, 35, 146, 224, 276, 279, 322, 327, 328, 389, 586, 588, 593, 622, 682, 684, 718, 721, 726, 737, 810, 891, 909, 931, 949, 1014, 1025, 1054, 1066, 1095, 1097, 1120, 1141, 1255, 1282, 1286, 1333, 1375, 1452, 1516, 1549, 1555, 1556, 1563, 1582, 1694, 1714, 1802, 1846, 1900; on the other hand, 834 (*usually* but then). *Cf.* then.
thanke, thanks, gratitude, 794.
that, that which, what, 54, 438, 1864; *redundant*, 88.
the, thee, 300, 388, 391, 406, 597, 787, 1151, 1153, 1154, 1511, 1563, 1605, 1830; **for* thou, 1016.
thee, the, 1364.
thee, thrive, fare, 715; 'ill a t.', 678, 'evill a t.', 1813, ill betide him.
then, than, 78 (thenne), 154, 288, 519, 658, 748, 771, 993, 994, 1134, 1136, 1170, 1426, 1589, 1595, 1733, 1839.
then, then, 113, 188, 194, 375, 530, 590, 1016, 1128, 1238, 1606, 1837; on the other hand, 1465 (*usually* but then). *Cf.* than.
therwhile, meanwhile, 1657.
*thick, thiek, the ilk, the very; 'thiek', 697; 'thicke same', 685; 'thickesame', 1595; 'thieke same', 688; 'thieke same way goeth the hare', that is how the matter stands, 674.
*thissame, 999, 1031, 1067, 1087.
thrifte, fortune *or* earnings, 989, 1852.
thrihumphe, triumph, 1472 (? assimilated to θρίαμβος; trihumph *is elsewhere recorded*).
thrist, thirst, 896, 1343; distress, 1382.
thyll, the ill, 1418.
tigither, together, 1059.
to, towards, in the pursuit of, 127; compared with, 534.
to, too, 800, 1016, 1849.

*tone, the one, 696.
too, to, 585, 1886, 1887, 1931.
tooke . . . vppon, *see under* take vppon.
tooting, peeping, prying, 159.
*toritee, *for* authority, 1805.
*torment (I torment), *past part.*, tormented, tortured, 649.
*tother, the other, 696.
tottering, swinging, hanging, 1841 (tottered *is also a common variant of* tattered, *hence the assoc. with* rags).
towarde, on the way to, 1126; in contemplation, planned, 1552; impending, 1640.
towch (of), touch upon, speak of, 15.
toyes, trifles (*here* purses), 476.
trade, a course, practice, 525.
traine, for a, 1603, *explained as* for a while *in* O.E.D.; *but rather* as a stratagem *or* trap (*see* 1609, 1612); 'for atraine', as a decoy, 1665.
travaile, to labour, endeavour, 720.
trawth, troth, truth, 462.
tripth, trippeth, stumbles, 562 (*cf.* 414).
*trounst (I trounst), trounced, afflicted, harassed, 651.
trowe, trow ye, ween ye, 997, 1667 (*cf.* trowe youe, 1290).
trumperye, fraud, imposture, 1743.
trussing corda (*punningly*) hanging rope, halter; 'plaie een plaine t. c.', be hanged, 1324 (Misericordia *without the* i's *is* miser corda, wretched hearts, *or* (*for* chorda) wretched rope).
truste, trustiness, 279; 'best be t.', *prob. for* best betrust, best trusted, 343; 'of t.', truly, 1564.
trye owte, to examine, sift, 1236.
tryppe, take . . . in a, to catch tripping, detect in an error, 1713 (*perh. misunderstood as* take in a trap).
tuff, tuffa, *an exclamation imitative of an escape of breath*, 247; tuffing, puffing, 773.
tuffet, tuft, 927.
*twaie, twain, two, 1082.
twigg, a shoot, youngster, 339.
twigge, to whip, 1630.

GLOSSARY

tyme, opportunity, 255; a limited period, 901; 't. trieth all', 27.

Þ

*Used only in People's part as the initial letter of þee, 678, 715, 1813; þey, 1166; þicke, 688; þieke, 674, 685, 697; þinges, 668; þinke, 658, 660; þynke, 656; þought, 1165. The words are glossed (when necessary) under th.

U V

*vaine, fain, obliged, 1082.
*valeslye, falsely, 638.
*vast, fast; 'goddes v.', Christ's fasting, 1777.
*vaye, 1014; vei, 665; vey, 1778; fay, faith.
vengeaunce, 'with a v.', a curse on you, 1626.
*venter, venture, 1578.
verai, veray, adj., very, actual, 71, 198.
verai, adv., very, truly, 195.
verament, verily, indeed, 1233.
Veritas de terra orta est, 1706, see Psal. lxxxiv. 12 (A.V. lxxxv. 11).
vertue, power, 1756.
*vet, fet, fetched, 1016.
vncorrecte, past part., uncorrected, 51.
vnderstand, hear of, 970.
vngracious, graceless, unfortunate, 907.
vnhappie, causing misfortune, unchancy, 910.
vntill, vntyll, to; 'putt v.', set to, 545; 'saie vs v.', say to us, 1062.
*vole, foal, 1023.
*vorst, first, 678.
vouchesalve, vouchsafe, 1405.
vprightlie, with strict justice, 1901.
vsiree, usury, 1740.
vtmoste, outer, 1773.

W

waite, weight, 284.
*waite avore youe, attend on you before (like an usher), 739.
waives, waifs; 'w. and straies', ownerless or unclaimed property, 97.

*warte, for warrant, 639, 721, 1812.
wast, was't, was it, 1290.
waste, in, in vain, 1442.
watier, water, 762.
waye, 'in the w. of your goodspede', by way of (or as an instance of) well wishing, 1437.
weale, wealth, welfare (regularly in the comp. Common weale), 19 et passim.
well, fitly, 324.
we(a)lth(e), wealth, riches, 799; well-being, good condition, 1331, 1427, &c.
wemme, blemish, 565.
weorke, sb., work, 733, 1543 (but worke, 1242).
weorke, vb., to work; act, proceed, 695, 1000, 1834; commit, 86; cause, 1648.
were, wear, 780.
Westminster hale, the law courts, 1595.
whan, when, 21, 269, 318, 429, 589, 650, 718, 878, 893, 937, 997, 1027, 1041, 1070, 1077, 1080, 1101, 1149, 1172, 1185, 1192, 1265, 1337, 1343, 1383, 1417, 1445, 1480, 1528, 1643, 1689, 1691, 1754, 1822, 1918. Cf. when.
whare, where, 640; whether, 712. Cf. where.
what, whatever, 356; what for, why, 613, 1577; interj., 779; 'w. any', what single, 729.
what is the clock, see under Iohn holde my stafe.
wheale, pustule, 'a w. of', disease light upon, 163.
when, when, 218, 268, 281, 329, 433, 838, 1535. Cf. whan.
where, whether, 1050. Cf. whare.
whether, whither, 1659, 1667, 1810.
while the grasse shall growe the horse shall sterve, 1120.
whipp(e), 'on the w.', obscure, original defective, 1714; 'w. over the chaine', skip, 1755.
whitt, whytt, scrap, jot, 698; and see under 'as good'.
whoughe, interj., how, 721.
whowe, adv., how, 475.

GLOSSARY 83

whretch, *aberrant spelling of* wretch, *perh. a miswriting*, 1051.
*widge, mare, 1023.
*win (ichwin), ween, 1084.
wincheth, kicks, proves recalcitrant, 284.
winde, breath, 1632.
winke, to sleep, 1135; to close the eyes, 1164.
wissed, wished, 2; wisshed, 1005.
with, ? belonging to, 1849.
wo, for, to the point of hurting, 770.
woodenes, madness, 1173.
worthe, wo, ill befall, a curse on, 121.
woulff, wolf; 'a w. in the tale' (*lupus in fabula*), speak of the devil, 749.
woundes, by his, by God's wounds, 130. *Cf.* armes.
*wrong, wrung, oppressed, 649.
wrong contribution, extortion, 1898.
wrowte, wrought, 1539.

Y

yche, *see* iche.
ye, yea (*perh. a miswriting*), 1120, 1848.
yeare, ? *error for* geare, 612; 'for the next y.', for what may happen in the future, 1572.
yearthe, earth, 1190, 1360; yearethlye, earthly, 439.
yei, eye, 474; yeis, 1214.
*yele, ye'll, ye will, 1163.
yet, *see* for yet.
yls, ills, 51.
yong, young, early (days), 730.
youe will over the hedge ere ye come att the stile, you are in too great a hurry, 262.
yst, is't, is it, 353.

Z

*zedge, say, 1590.
*zelie, seely, simple, 660.
zelosie, zelousye (*from* zealous), jealousy, mistrust, 995, 1771.
*zemlitee, *for* semblety (*from* semble, like), 'of z.', seemingly, 1044.
*zorowe, with, with sorrow, *an imprecation*, 663.
*zorylesse, *for* insolence, 688.

ADDITIONAL GLOSSES

affection, partiality, 1783.
as, in such manner as, 264.
carpenters weorke, ? a neat job, 1543.
case, need, 1927 (*app. an extension of the sense of* plight).
hoe, ho (*exclamation*), 1165.
manior, manor, 784.
masse, mass, structure, 1189.
putte backe, discarded, 491.
shaken, of, renounced, 491.
singuler, particular, personal, 1133.
throod, the rood, the cross, 1035.
tyll, 1610, *used in place of* to *with inf.* (*mainly Sc.*), *but here app. doing duty for* till to.

EARLY ENGLISH TEXT SOCIETY

OFFICERS AND COUNCIL

Honorary Director
Professor NORMAN DAVIS, Merton College, Oxford

Professor J. A. W. BENNETT
R. W. BURCHFIELD
Professor BRUCE DICKINS, F.B.A.
Professor E. J. DOBSON
A. I. DOYLE
Professor P. HODGSON
Professor G. KANE

Miss P. M. KEAN
N. R. KER, F.B.A.
Professor J. R. R. TOLKIEN
Professor D. WHITELOCK, F.B.A.
Professor R. M. WILSON
Professor C. L. WRENN

Editorial Secretary
Dr. P. O. E. GRADON, St. Hugh's College, Oxford

Executive Secretary
Dr. A. M. HUDSON, Lady Margaret Hall, Oxford

Bankers
THE NATIONAL PROVINCIAL BANK LTD., Cornmarket Street, Oxford

THE Subscription to the Society, which constitutes full membership for private members and libraries, is £3. 3s. (U.S. and Canadian members $9.00) a year for the annual publications, due in advance on the 1st of JANUARY, and should be paid by Cheque, Postal Order, or Money Order made out to 'The Early English Text Society', to Dr. A. M. Hudson, Executive Secretary, Early English Text Society, Lady Margaret Hall, Oxford.

The payment of the annual subscription is the only prerequisite of membership.

Private members of the Society (but not libraries) may select other volumes of the Society's publications instead of those for the current year. The value of texts allowed against one annual subscription is 100s. (U.S. members 110s.), and all such transactions must be made through the Executive Secretary.

Members of the Society (including institutional members) may also, through the Executive Secretary, purchase copies of past E.E.T.S. publications and reprints for their own use at a discount of 4d. in the shilling.

The Society's texts are also available to non-members at listed prices through any bookseller.

The Society's texts are published by the Oxford University Press.

The Early English Text Society was founded in 1864 by Frederick James Furnivall, with the help of Richard Morris, Walter Skeat, and others, to bring the mass of unprinted Early English literature within the reach of students and provide sound texts from which the New English Dictionary could quote. In 1867 an Extra Series was started of texts already printed but not in satisfactory or readily obtainable editions.

In 1921 the Extra Series was discontinued and all the publications of 1921 and subsequent years have since been listed and numbered as part of the Original Series. Since 1921 just over a hundred new volumes have been issued; and since 1957 alone more than a hundred and thirty volumes have been reprinted at a cost of £65,000.

In this prospectus the Original Series and Extra Series for the years 1867–1920 are amalgamated, so as to show all the publications of the Society in a single list.

From 1 April 1969, since many of the old prices had become uneconomic in modern publishing conditions, a new price structure was introduced and the new prices are shown in this list. From the same date the discount allowed to members was increased from 2d. in the shilling to 4d. in the shilling.

LIST OF PUBLICATIONS

Original Series, 1864–1969. Extra Series, 1867–1920

O.S.	1. Early English Alliterative Poems, ed. R. Morris. (*Reprinted* 1965.) 54s.	1864
	2. Arthur, ed. F. J. Furnivall. (*Reprinted* 1965.) 10s.	,,
	3. Lauder on the Dewtie of Kyngis, &c., 1556, ed. F. Hall. (*Reprinted* 1965.) 18s.	,,
	4. Sir Gawayne and the Green Knight, ed. R. Morris. (*Out of print, see* O.S. 210.)	
	5. Hume's Orthographie and Congruitie of the Britan Tongue, ed. H. B. Wheatley. (*Reprinted* 1965.) 18s.	1865
	6. Lancelot of the Laik, ed. W. W. Skeat. (*Reprinted* 1965.) 42s.	,,
	7. Genesis & Exodus, ed. R. Morris. (*Out of print.*)	,,
	8. Morte Arthure, ed. E. Brock. (*Reprinted* 1967.) 25s.	,,
	9. Thynne on Speght's ed. of Chaucer, A.D. 1599, ed. G. Kingsley and F. J. Furnivall. (*Reprinted* 1965.) 55s.	,,
	10. Merlin, Part I, ed. H. B. Wheatley. (*Out of print.*)	,,
	11. Lyndesay's Monarche, &c., ed. J. Small. Part I. (*Out of print.*)	,,
	12. The Wright's Chaste Wife, ed. F. J. Furnivall. (*Reprinted* 1965.) 10s.	,,
	13. Seinte Marherete, ed. O. Cockayne. (*Out of print, see* O.S. 193.)	1866
	14. King Horn, Floriz and Blauncheflur, &c., ed. J. R. Lumby, re-ed. G. H. McKnight. (*Reprinted* 1962.) 50s.	
	15. Political, Religious, and Love Poems, ed. F. J. Furnivall. (*Reprinted* 1965.) 63s.	,,
	16. The Book of Quinte Essence, ed. F. J. Furnivall. (*Reprinted* 1965.) 10s.	,,
	17. Parallel Extracts from 45 MSS. of Piers the Plowman, ed. W. W. Skeat. (*Out of print.*)	,,
	18. Hali Meidenhad, ed. O. Cockayne, re-ed. F. J. Furnivall. (*Out of print.*)	,,
	19. Lyndesay's Monarche, &c., ed. J. Small. Part II. (*Out of print.*)	,,
	20. Richard Rolle de Hampole, English Prose Treatises of, ed. G. G. Perry. (*Out of print.*)	,,
	21. Merlin, ed. H. B. Wheatley. Part II. (*Out of print.*)	,,
	22. Partenay or Lusignen, ed. W. W. Skeat. (*Out of print.*)	,,
	23. Dan Michel's Ayenbite of Inwyt, ed. R. Morris and P. Gradon. Vol. I, Text. (*Reissued* 1965.) 54s.	,,
	24. Hymns to the Virgin and Christ; The Parliament of Devils, &c., ed. F. J. Furnivall. (*Out of print.*)	1867
	25. The Stacions of Rome, the Pilgrims' Sea-voyage, with Clene Maydenhod, ed. F. J. Furnivall. (*Out of print.*)	,,
	26. Religious Pieces in Prose and Verse, from R. Thornton's MS., ed. G. G. Perry. (*See under* 1913.) (*Out of print.*)	,,
	27. Levins' Manipulus Vocabulorum, a rhyming Dictionary, ed. H. B. Wheatley. (*Out of print.*)	,,
	28. William's Vision of Piers the Plowman, ed. W. W. Skeat. A-Text. (*Reprinted* 1968.) 35s.	
	29. Old English Homilies (1220–30), ed. R. Morris. Series I, Part I. (*Out of print.*)	,,
	30. Pierce the Ploughmans Crede, ed. W. W. Skeat. (*Out of print.*)	,,
E.S.	1. William of Palerne or William and the Werwolf, re-ed. W. W. Skeat. (*Out of print.*)	
	2. Early English Pronunciation, by A. J. Ellis. Part I. (*Out of print.*)	,,
O.S.	31. Myrc's Duties of a Parish Priest, in Verse, ed. E. Peacock. (*Out of print.*)	1868
	32. Early English Meals and Manners: the Boke of Norture of John Russell, the Bokes of Keruynge, Curtasye, and Demeanor, the Babees Book, Urbanitatis, &c., ed. F. J. Furnivall. (*Out of print.*)	,,
	33. The Book of the Knight of La Tour-Landry, ed. T. Wright. (*Out of print.*)	,,
	34. Old English Homilies (before 1300), ed. R. Morris. Series I, Part II. (*Out of print.*)	,,
	35. Lyndesay's Works, Part III: The Historie and Testament of Squyer Meldrum, ed. F. Hall. (*Reprinted* 1965.) 18s.	,,
E.S.	3. Caxton's Book of Curtesye, in Three Versions, ed. F. J. Furnivall. (*Out of print.*)	,,
	4. Havelok the Dane, re-ed. W. W. Skeat. (*Out of print.*)	,,
	5. Chaucer's Boethius, ed. R. Morris. (*Reprinted* 1969.) 40s.	,,
	6. Chevelere Assigne, re-ed. Lord Aldenham. (*Out of print.*)	,,
O.S.	36. Merlin, ed. H. B. Wheatley. Part III. On Arthurian Localities, by J. S. Stuart Glennie. (*Out of print.*)	1869
	37. Sir David Lyndesay's Works, Part IV, Ane Satyre of the thrie Estaits, ed. F. Hall. (*Out of print.*)	,,
	38. William's Vision of Piers the Plowman, ed. W. W. Skeat. Part II. Text B. (*Reprinted* 1964.) 42s.	,,
	39, 56. The Gest Hystoriale of the Destruction of Troy, ed. D. Donaldson and G. A. Panton. Parts I and II. (*Reprinted as one volume* 1968.) 110s.	,,
E.S.	7. Early English Pronunciation, by A. J. Ellis. Part II. (*Out of print.*)	
	8. Queene Elizabethes Achademy, &c., ed. F. J. Furnivall. Essays on early Italian and German Books of Courtesy, by W. M. Rossetti and E. Oswald. (*Out of print.*)	,,
	9. Awdeley's Fraternitye of Vacabondes, Harman's Caveat, &c., ed. E. Viles and F. J. Furnivall. (*Out of print.*)	,,
O.S.	40. English Gilds, their Statutes and Customs, A.D. 1389, ed. Toulmin Smith and Lucy T. Smith, with an Essay on Gilds and Trades-Unions, by L. Brentano. (*Reprinted* 1963.) 100s.	1870
	41. William Lauder's Minor Poems, ed. F. J. Furnivall. (*Out of print.*)	,,
	42. Bernardus De Cura Rei Famuliaris, Early Scottish Prophecies, &c., ed. J. R. Lumby. (*Reprinted* 1965.) 18s.	
	43. Ratis Raving, and other Moral and Religious Pieces, ed. J. R. Lumby. (*Out of print.*)	,,
E.S.	10. Andrew Boorde's Introduction of Knowledge, 1547, Dyetary of Helth, 1542, Barnes in Defence of the Berde, 1542-3, ed. F. J. Furnivall. (*Out of print.*)	,,
	11, 55. Barbour's Bruce, ed. W. W. Skeat. Parts I and IV. (*Reprinted as Volume I* 1968.) 63s.	,,
O.S.	44. The Alliterative Romance of Joseph of Arimathie, or The Holy Grail: from the Vernon MS.; with W. de Worde's and Pynson's Lives of Joseph: ed. W. W. Skeat. (*Out of print.*)	1871

O.S. 45.	King Alfred's West-Saxon Version of Gregory's Pastoral Care, ed., with an English translation, by Henry Sweet. Part I. *(Reprinted 1958.)* 55s.	1871
46.	Legends of the Holy Rood, Symbols of the Passion and Cross Poems, ed. R. Morris. *(Out of print.)*	,,
47.	Sir David Lyndesay's Works, ed. J. A. H. Murray. Part V. *(Out of print.)*	,,
48.	The Times' Whistle, and other Poems, by R. C., 1616; ed. J. M. Cowper. *(Out of print.)*	,,
E.S. 12.	England in Henry VIII's Time: a Dialogue between Cardinal Pole and Lupset, by Thom. Starkey, Chaplain to Henry VIII, ed. J. M. Cowper. Part II. *(Out of print,* Part I is E.S. 32, 1878.)	,,
13.	A Supplicacyon of the Beggers, by Simon Fish, A.D. 1528–9, ed. F. J. Furnivall, with A Supplication to our Moste Soueraigne Lorde, A Supplication of the Poore Commons, and The Decaye of England by the Great Multitude of Sheep, ed. J. M. Cowper. *(Out of print.)*	,,
14.	Early English Pronunciation, by A. J. Ellis. Part III. *(Out of print.)*	,,
O.S. 49.	An Old English Miscellany, containing a Bestiary, Kentish Sermons, Proverbs of Alfred, and Religious Poems of the 13th cent., ed. R. Morris. *(Out of print.)*	1872
50.	King Alfred's West-Saxon Version of Gregory's Pastoral Care, ed. H. Sweet. Part II. *(Reprinted 1958.)* 50s.	,,
51.	Þe Liflade of St. Juliana, 2 versions, with translations, ed. O. Cockayne and E. Brock. *(Reprinted 1957.)* 38s.	,,
52.	Palladius on Husbondrie, englisht, ed. Barton Lodge. Part I. *(Out of print.)*	,,
E.S. 15.	Robert Crowley's Thirty-One Epigrams, Voyce of the Last Trumpet, Way to Wealth, &c., ed. J. M. Cowper. *(Out of print.)*	,,
16.	Chaucer's Treatise on the Astrolabe, ed. W. W. Skeat. *(Reprinted 1969.)* 40s.	,,
17.	The Complaynt of Scotlande, with 4 Tracts, ed. J. A. H. Murray. Part I. *(Out of print.)*	,,
O.S. 53.	Old-English Homilies, Series II, and three Hymns to the Virgin and God, 13th-century, with the music to two of them, in old and modern notation, ed. R. Morris. *(Out of print.)*	1873
54.	The Vision of Piers Plowman, ed. W. W. Skeat. Part III. Text C. *(Reprinted 1959.)* 55s.	,,
55.	Generydes, a Romance, ed. W. Aldis Wright. Part I. *(Out of print.)*	,,
E.S. 18.	The Complaynt of Scotlande, ed. J. A. H. Murray. Part II. *(Out of print.)*	,,
19.	The Myroure of oure Ladye, ed. J. H. Blunt. *(Out of print.)*	,,
O.S. 56.	The Gest Hystoriale of the Destruction of Troy, in alliterative verse, ed. D. Donaldson and G. A. Panton. Part II. *(See* O.S. 39.)	1874
57.	Cursor Mundi, in four Texts, ed. R. Morris. Part I. *(Reprinted 1961.)* 40s.	,,
58, 63, 73.	The Blickling Homilies, ed. R. Morris. Parts I, II, and III. *(Reprinted as one volume 1967.)* 70s.	,,
E.S. 20.	Lovelich's History of the Holy Grail, ed. F. J. Furnivall. Part I. *(Out of print.)*	,,
21, 29.	Barbour's Bruce, ed. W. W. Skeat. Parts II and III. *(Reprinted as Volume II* 1968.) 90s.	
22.	Henry Brinklow's Complaynt of Roderyck Mors and The Lamentacyon of a Christen Agaynst the Cytye of London, made by Roderigo Mors, ed. J. M. Cowper. *(Out of print.)*	,,
23.	Early English Pronunciation, by A. J. Ellis. Part IV. *(Out of print.)*	,,
O.S. 59.	Cursor Mundi, in four Texts, ed. R. Morris. Part II. *(Reprinted 1966.)* 50s.	1875
60.	Meditacyuns on the Soper of our Lorde, by Robert of Brunne, ed. J. M. Cowper. *(Out of print.)*	,,
61.	The Romance and Prophecies of Thomas of Erceldoune, ed. J. A. H. Murray. *(Out of print.)*	,,
E.S. 24.	Lovelich's History of the Holy Grail, ed. F. J. Furnivall. Part II. *(Out of print.)*	,,
25, 26.	Guy of Warwick, 15th-century Version, ed. J. Zupitza. Pts. I and II. *(Reprinted as one volume 1966.)* 75s.	
O.S. 62.	Cursor Mundi, in four Texts, ed. R. Morris. Part III. *(Reprinted 1966.)* 40s.	1876
63.	The Blickling Homilies, ed. R. Morris. Part II. *(See* O.S. 58.)	,,
64.	Francis Thynne's Embleames and Epigrams, ed. F. J. Furnivall. *(Out of print.)*	,,
65.	Be Domes Dæge (Bede's *De Die Judicii*), &c., ed. J. R. Lumby. *(Reprinted* 1964.) 30s.	,,
E.S. 26.	Guy of Warwick, 15th-century Version, ed. J. Zupitza. Part II. *(See* E.S. 25.)	,,
27.	The English Works of John Fisher, ed. J. E. B. Mayor. Part I. *(Out of print.)*	,,
O.S. 66.	Cursor Mundi, in four Texts, ed. R. Morris. Part IV. *(Reprinted* 1966.) 40s.	1877
67.	Notes on Piers Plowman, by W. W. Skeat. Part I. *(Out of print.)*	,,
E.S. 28.	Lovelich's Holy Grail, ed. F. J. Furnivall. Part III. *(Out of print.)*	,,
29.	Barbour's Bruce, ed. W. W. Skeat. Part III. *(See* E.S. 21.)	,,
O.S. 68.	Cursor Mundi, in 4 Texts, ed. R. Morris. Part V. *(Reprinted* 1966.) 40s.	1878
69.	Adam Davie's 5 Dreams about Edward II, &c., ed. F. J. Furnivall. 30s.	,,
70.	Generydes, a Romance, ed. W. Aldis Wright. Part II. *(Out of print.)*	,,
E.S. 30.	Lovelich's Holy Grail, ed. F. J. Furnivall. Part IV. *(Out of print.)*	,,
31.	The Alliterative Romance of Alexander and Dindimus, ed. W. W. Skeat. *(Out of print.)*	,,
32.	Starkey's England in Henry VIII's Time. Part I. Starkey's Life and Letters, ed. S. J. Herrtage. *(Out of print.)*	,,
O.S. 71.	The Lay Folks Mass-Book, four texts, ed. T. F. Simmons. *(Reprinted* 1968.) 90s.	1879
72.	Palladius on Husbondrie, englisht, ed. S. J. Herrtage. Part II. 42s.	,,
E.S. 33.	Gesta Romanorum, ed. S. J. Herrtage. *(Reprinted* 1962.) 100s.	,,
34.	The Charlemagne Romances; 1, Sir Ferumbras, from Ashm. MS. 33, ed. S. J. Herrtage. *(Reprinted* 1966.) 54s.	,,
O.S. 73.	The Blickling Homilies, ed. R. Morris. Part III. *(See* O.S. 58.)	1880
74.	English Works of Wyclif, hitherto unprinted, ed. F. D. Matthew. *(Out of print.)*	,,
E.S. 35.	Charlemagne Romances: 2. The Sege of Melayne, Sir Otuell, &c., ed. S. J. Herrtage. *(Out of print.)*	,,
36, 37.	Charlemagne Romances: 3 and 4. Lyf of Charles the Grete, ed. S. J. Herrtage. Parts I and II. *(Reprinted as one volume* 1967.) 54s.	,,
O.S. 75.	Catholicon Anglicum, an English-Latin Wordbook, from Lord Monson's MS., A.D. 1483, ed., with Introduction and Notes, by S. J. Herrtage and Preface by H. B. Wheatley. *(Out of print.)*	1881
76, 82.	Ælfric's Lives of Saints, in MS. Cott. Jul. E VII, ed. W. W. Skeat. Parts I and II. *(Reprinted as Volume I* 1966.) 60s.	,,

3

E.S. 37.	Charlemagne Romances: 4. Lyf of Charles the Grete, ed. S. J. Herrtage. Part II. (*See* E.S. 36.)	1881
38.	Charlemagne Romances: 5. The Sowdone of Babylone, ed. E. Hausknecht. (*Out of print.*)	,,
O.S. 77.	Beowulf, the unique MS. autotyped and transliterated, ed. J. Zupitza. (*Re-issued as* No. 245. *See under* 1958.)	1882
78.	The Fifty Earliest English Wills, in the Court of Probate, 1387–1439, ed. F. J. Furnivall. (*Reprinted* 1964.) 50s.	,,
E.S. 39.	Charlemagne Romances: 6. Rauf Coilyear, Roland, Otuel, &c., ed. S. J. Herrtage. (*Out of print.*)	,,
40.	Charlemagne Romances: 7. Huon of Burdeux, by Lord Berners, ed. S. L. Lee. Part I. (*Out of print.*)	,,
O.S. 79.	King Alfred's Orosius, from Lord Tollemache's 9th-century MS., ed. H. Sweet. Part I. (*Reprinted* 1959.) 55s.	1883
79 b.	Extra Volume. Facsimile of the Epinal Glossary, ed. H. Sweet. (*Out of print.*)	,,
E.S. 41.	Charlemagne Romances: 8. Huon of Burdeux, by Lord Berners, ed. S. L. Lee. Part II. (*Out of print.*)	,,
42, 49, 59.	Guy of Warwick: 2 texts (Auchinleck MS. and Caius MS.), ed. J. Zupitza. Parts I, II, and III. (*Reprinted as one volume* 1966). 110s.	,,
O.S. 80.	The Life of St. Katherine, B.M. Royal MS. 17 A. xxvii, &c., and its Latin Original, ed. E. Einenkel. (*Out of print.*)	1884
81.	Piers Plowman: Glossary, &c., ed. W. W. Skeat. Part IV, completing the work. (*Out of print.*)	,,
E.S. 43.	Charlemagne Romances: 9. Huon of Burdeux, by Lord Berners, ed. S. L. Lee. Part III. (*Out of print.*)	,,
44.	Charlemagne Romances: 10. The Foure Sonnes of Aymon, ed. Octavia Richardson. Part I. (*Out of print.*)	,,
O.S. 82.	Ælfric's Lives of Saints, MS. Cott. Jul. E vii ed. W. W. Skeat. Part II. (*See* O.S. 76.)	1885
83.	The Oldest English Texts, Charters, &c., ed. H. Sweet. (*Reprinted* 1966.) 110s.	,,
E.S. 45.	Charlemagne Romances: 11. The Foure Sonnes of Aymon, ed. O. Richardson. Part II. (*Out of print.*)	,,
46.	Sir Beves of Hamtoun, ed. E. Kölbing. Part I. (*Out of print.*)	,,
O.S. 84.	Additional Analogs to 'The Wright's Chaste Wife', O.S. 12, by W. A. Clouston. (*Out of print.*)	1886
85.	The Three Kings of Cologne, ed. C. Horstmann. (*Out of print.*)	,,
86.	Prose Lives of Women Saints, ed. C. Horstmann. (*Out of print.*)	,,
E.S. 47.	The Wars of Alexander, ed. W. W. Skeat. (*Out of print.*)	,,
48.	Sir Beves of Hamtoun, ed. E. Kölbing. Part II. (*Out of print.*)	,,
O.S. 87.	The Early South-English Legendary, Laud MS. 108, ed. C. Hortsmann. (*Out of print.*)	1887
88.	Hy. Bradshaw's Life of St. Werburghe (Pynson, 1521), ed. C. Horstmann. (*Out of print.*)	,,
E.S. 49.	Guy of Warwick, 2 texts (Auchinleck and Caius MSS.), ed. J. Zupitza. Part II. (*See* E.S. 42.)	,,
50.	Charlemagne Romances: 12. Huon of Burdeux, by Lord Berners, ed. S. L. Lee. Part IV. (*Out of print.*)	,,
51.	Torrent of Portyngale, ed. E. Adam. (*Out of print.*)	,,
O.S. 89.	Vices and Virtues, ed. F. Holthausen. Part I. (*Reprinted* 1967.) 40s.	1888
90.	Anglo-Saxon and Latin Rule of St. Benet, interlinear Glosses, ed. H. Logeman. (*Out of print.*)	,,
91.	Two Fifteenth-Century Cookery-Books, ed. T. Austin. (*Reprinted* 1964.) 42s.	,,
E.S. 52.	Bullein's Dialogue against the Feuer Pestilence, 1578, ed. M. and A. H. Bullen. (*Out of print.*)	,,
53.	Vicary's Anatomie of the Body of Man, 1548, ed. 1577, ed. F. J. and Percy Furnivall. Part I. (*Out of print.*)	,,
54.	The Curial made by maystere Alain Charretier, translated by William Caxton, 1484, ed. F. J. Furnivall and P. Meyer. (*Reprinted* 1965.) 13s.	,,
O.S. 92.	Eadwine's Canterbury Psalter, from the Trin. Cambr. MS., ed. F. Harsley, Part II. (*Out of print.*)	1889
93.	Defensor's Liber Scintillarum, ed. E. Rhodes. (*Out of print.*)	,,
E.S. 55.	Barbour's Bruce, ed. W. W. Skeat. Part IV. (*See* E.S. 11.)	,,
56.	Early English Pronunciation, by A. J. Ellis. Part V, the present English Dialects. (*Out of print.*)	,,
O.S. 94, 114.	Ælfric's Lives of Saints, MS. Cott. Jul. E vii, ed. W. W. Skeat. Parts III and IV. (*Reprinted as Volume II* 1966.) 60s.	1890
95.	The Old-English Version of Bede's Ecclesiastical History, re-ed. T. Miller. Part I, 1. (*Reprinted* 1959.) 54s.	,,
E.S. 57.	Caxton's Eneydos, ed. W. T. Culley and F. J. Furnivall. (*Reprinted* 1962.) 50s.	,,
58.	Caxton's Blanchardyn and Eglantine, c. 1489, ed. L. Kellner. (*Reprinted* 1962.) 63s.	,,
O.S. 96.	The Old-English Version of Bede's Ecclesiastical History, re-ed. T. Miller. Part I, 2. (*Reprinted* 1959.) 54s.	1891
97.	The Earliest English Prose Psalter, ed. K. D. Buelbring. Part I. (*Out of print.*)	,,
E.S. 59.	Guy of Warwick, 2 texts (Auchinleck and Caius MSS.), ed. J. Zupitza. Part III. (*See* E.S. 42.)	,,
60.	Lydgate's Temple of Glas, re-ed. J. Schick. (*Out of print.*)	,,
O.S. 98.	Minor Poems of the Vernon MS., ed. C. Horstmann. Part I. (*Out of print.*)	1892
99.	Cursor Mundi. Preface, Notes, and Glossary, Part VI, ed. R. Morris. (*Reprinted* 1962.) 35s.	,,
E.S. 61.	Hoccleve's Minor Poems, I, from the Phillipps and Durham MSS., ed. F. J. Furnivall. (*Out of print.*)	,,
62.	The Chester Plays, re-ed. H. Deimling. Part I. (*Reprinted* 1967.) 38s.	,,
O.S. 100.	Capgrave's Life of St. Katharine, ed. C. Horstmann, with Forewords by F. J. Furnivall. (*Out of print.*)	1893
O.S. 101.	Cursor Mundi. Essay on the MSS., their Dialects, &c., by H. Hupe. Part VII. (*Reprinted* 1962.) 35s.	,,
E.S. 63.	Thomas à Kempis's De Imitatione Christi, ed. J. K. Ingram. (*Out of print.*)	,,
64.	Caxton's Godeffroy of Boloyne, or The Siege and Conqueste of Jerusalem, 1481, ed. Mary N. Colvin. (*Out of print.*)	,,
O.S. 102.	Lanfranc's Science of Cirurgie, ed. R. von Fleischhacker. Part I. (*Out of print.*)	1894

O.S. 103. The Legend of the Cross, &c., ed. A. S. Napier. (*Out of print.*)	1894	
E.S. 65. Sir Beves of Hamtoun, ed. E. Kölbing. Part III. (*Out of print.*)	,,	
66. Lydgate's and Burgh's Secrees of Philisoffres ('Governance of Kings and Princes'), ed. R. Steele. (*Out of print.*)	,,	
O.S. 104. The Exeter Book (Anglo-Saxon Poems), re-ed. I. Gollancz. Part I. (*Reprinted 1958.*) 55s.	1895	
105. The Prymer or Lay Folks' Prayer Book, Camb. Univ. MS., ed. H. Littlehales. Part I. (*Out of print.*)	,,	
E.S. 67. The Three Kings' Sons, a Romance, ed. F. J. Furnivall. Part I, the Text. (*Out of print.*)	,,	
68. Melusine, the prose Romance, ed. A. K. Donald. Part I, the Text. (*Out of print.*)	,,	
O.S. 106. R. Misyn's Fire of Love and Mending of Life (Hampole), ed. R. Harvey. (*Out of print.*)	1896	
107. The English Conquest of Ireland, A.D. 1166–1185, 2 Texts, ed. F. J. Furnivall. Part I. (*Out of print.*)	,,	
E.S. 69. Lydgate's Assembly of the Gods, ed. O. L. Triggs. (*Reprinted 1957.*) 42s.	,,	
70. The Digby Plays, ed. F. J. Furnivall. (*Reprinted 1967.*) 30s.	,,	
O.S. 108. Child-Marriages and -Divorces, Trothplights, &c. Chester Depositions, 1561–6, ed. F. J. Furnivall. (*Out of print.*)	1897	
109. The Prymer or Lay Folks' Prayer Book, ed. H. Littlehales. Part II. (*Out of print.*)	,,	
E.S. 71. The Towneley Plays, ed. G. England and A. W. Pollard. (*Reprinted 1966.*) 45s.	,,	
72. Hoccleve's Regement of Princes, and 14 Poems, ed. F. J. Furnivall. (*Out of print.*)	,,	
73. Hoccleve's Minor Poems, II, from the Ashburnham MS., ed. I. Gollancz. (*Out of print.*)	,,	
O.S. 110. The Old-English Version of Bede's Ecclesiastical History, ed. T. Miller. Part II, 1. (*Reprinted 1963.*) 55s.	1898	
111. The Old-English Version of Bede's Ecclesiastical History, ed. T. Miller. Part II, 2. (*Reprinted 1963.*) 55s.	,,	
E.S. 74. Secreta Secretorum, 3 prose Englishings, one by Jas. Yonge, 1428, ed. R. Steele. Part I. 55s.	,,	
75. Speculum Guidonis de Warwyk. ed. G. L. Morrill. (*Out of print.*)	,,	
O.S. 112. Merlin. Part IV. Outlines of the Legend of Merlin, by W. E. Mead. (*Out of print.*)	1899	
113. Queen Elizabeth's Englishings of Boethius, Plutarch, &c., ed. C. Pemberton. (*Out of print.*)	,,	
E.S. 76. George Ashby's Poems, &c., ed. Mary Bateson. (*Reprinted 1965.*) 30s.	,,	
77. Lydgate's DeGuilleville's Pilgrimage of the Life of Man, ed. F. J. Furnivall. Part I. (*Out of print.*)	,,	
78. The Life and Death of Mary Magdalene, by T. Robinson, *c.* 1620, ed. H. O. Sommer. 30s.	,,	
O.S. 114. Ælfric's Lives of Saints, ed. W. W. Skeat. Part IV and last. (*See* O.S. 94.)	1900	
115. Jacob's Well, ed. A. Brandeis. Part I. (*Out of print.*)	,,	
116. An Old-English Martyrology, re-ed. G. Herzfeld. (*Out of print.*)	,,	
E.S. 79. Caxton's Dialogues, English and French, ed. H. Bradley. (*Out of print.*)	,,	
80. Lydgate's Two Nightingale Poems, ed. O. Glauning. (*Out of print.*)	,,	
80A. Selections from Barbour's Bruce (Books I–X), ed. W. W. Skeat. (*Out of print.*)	,,	
81. The English Works of John Gower, ed. G. C. Macaulay. Part I. (*Reprinted 1957.*) 60s.	,,	
O.S. 117. Minor Poems of the Vernon MS., ed. F. J. Furnivall. Part II. (*Out of print.*)	1901	
118. The Lay Folks' Catechism, ed. T. F. Simmons and H. E. Nolloth. (*Out of print.*)	,,	
119. Robert of Brunne's Handlyng Synne, and its French original, re-ed. F. J. Furnivall. Part I. (*Out of print.*)	,,	
E.S. 82. The English Works of John Gower, ed. G. C. Macaulay. Part II. (*Reprinted 1957.*) 60s.	,,	
83. Lydgate's DeGuilleville's Pilgrimage of the Life of Man, ed. F. J. Furnivall. Part II. (*Out of print.*)	,,	
84. Lydgate's Reson and Sensuallyte, ed. E. Sieper. Vol. I. (*Reprinted 1965.*) 50s.	,,	
O.S. 120. The Rule of St. Benet in Northern Prose and Verse, and Caxton's Summary, ed. E. A. Kock. (*Out of print.*)	1902	
121. The Laud MS. Troy-Book, ed. J. E. Wülfing. Part I. (*Out of print.*)	,,	
E.S. 85. Alexander Scott's Poems, 1568, ed. A. K. Donald. (*Out of print.*)	,,	
86. William of Shoreham's Poems, re-ed. M. Konrath. Part I. (*Out of print.*)	,,	
87. Two Coventry Corpus Christi Plays, re-ed. H. Craig. (*See under* 1952.)	,,	
O.S. 122. The Laud MS. Troy-Book, ed. J. E. Wülfing. Part II. (*Out of print.*)	1903	
123. Robert of Brunne's Handlyng Synne, and its French original, re-ed. F. J. Furnivall. Part II. (*Out of print.*)	,,	
E.S. 88. Le Morte Arthur, re-ed. J. D. Bruce. (*Reprinted 1959.*) 45s.	,,	
89. Lydgate's Reson and Sensuallyte, ed. E. Sieper. Vol. II. (*Reprinted 1965.*) 35s.	,,	
90. English Fragments from Latin Medieval Service-Books, ed. H. Littlehales. (*Out of print.*)	,,	
O.S. 124. Twenty-six Political and other Poems from Digby MS. 102, &c., ed. J. Kail. Part I. 50s.	1904	
125. Medieval Records of a London City Church, ed. H. Littlehales. Part I. (*Out of print.*)	,,	
126. An Alphabet of Tales, in Northern English, from the Latin, ed. M. M. Banks. Part I. (*Out of print.*)	,,	
E.S. 91. The Macro Plays, ed. F. J. Furnivall and A. W. Pollard. (*Out of print*; see 262.)	,,	
92. Lydgate's DeGuilleville's Pilgrimage of the Life of Man, ed. Katherine B. Locock. Part III. (*Out of print.*)	,,	
93. Lovelich's Romance of Merlin, from the unique MS., ed. E. A. Kock. Part I. (*Out of print.*)	,,	
O.S. 127. An Alphabet of Tales, in Northern English, from the Latin, ed. M. M. Banks. Part II. (*Out of print.*)	1905	
128. Medieval Records of a London City Church, ed. H. Littlehales. Part II. (*Out of print.*)	,,	
129. The English Register of Godstow Nunnery, ed. A. Clark. Part I. 63s.	,,	
E.S. 94. Respublica, a Play on a Social England, ed. L. A. Magnus. (*Out of print. See under* 1946.)	,,	
95. Lovelich's History of the Holy Grail. Part V. The Legend of the Holy Grail, ed. Dorothy Kempe. (*Out of print.*)	,,	
96. Mirk's Festial, ed. T. Erbe. Part I. (*Out of print.*)	,,	
O.S. 130. The English Register of Godstow Nunnery, ed. A. Clark. Part II. 55s.	1906	
131. The Brut, or The Chronicle of England, ed. F. Brie. Part I. (*Reprinted 1960.*) 55s.	,,	
132. John Metham's Works, ed. H. Craig. 50s.	,,	
E.S. 97. Lydgate's Troy Book, ed. H. Bergen. Part I, Books I and II. (*Out of print.*)	,,	

E.S. 98.	Skelton's Magnyfycence, ed. R. L. Ramsay. *(Reprinted 1958.)* 55s.	1906
99.	The Romance of Emaré, re-ed. Edith Rickert. *(Reprinted 1958.)* 30s.	,,
O.S. 133.	The English Register of Oseney Abbey, by Oxford, ed. A. Clark. Part I. 50s.	1907
134.	The Coventry Leet Book, ed. M. Dormer Harris. Part I. *(Out of print.)*	,,
E.S. 100.	The Harrowing of Hell, and The Gospel of Nicodemus, re-ed. W. H. Hulme. *(Reprinted 1961.)* 50s.	
101.	Songs, Carols, &c., from Richard Hill's Balliol MS., ed. R. Dyboski. *(Out of print.)*	,,
O.S. 135.	The Coventry Leet Book, ed. M. Dormer Harris. Part II. *(Out of print.)*	1908
135 b.	*Extra Issue.* Prof. Manly's Piers Plowman and its Sequence, urging the fivefold authorship of the *Vision*. *(Out of print.)*	
136.	The Brut, or The Chronicle of England, ed. F. Brie. Part II. *(Out of print.)*	,,
E.S. 102.	Promptorium Parvulorum, the 1st English-Latin Dictionary, ed. A. L. Mayhew. *(Out of print.)*	,,
103.	Lydgate's Troy Book, ed. H. Bergen. Part II, Book III. *(Out of print.)*	,,
O.S. 137.	Twelfth-Century Homilies in MS. Bodley 343, ed. A. O. Belfour. Part I, the Text. *(Reprinted 1962.)* 28s.	1909
138.	The Coventry Leet Book, ed. M. Dormer Harris. Part III. *(Out of print.)*	,,
E.S. 104.	The Non-Cycle Mystery Plays, re-ed. O. Waterhouse. *(See end-note, p. 8.)*	,,
105.	The Tale of Beryn, with the Pardoner and Tapster, ed. F. J. Furnivall and W. G. Stone. *(Out of print.)*	,,
O.S. 139.	John Arderne's Treatises of Fistula in Ano, &c., ed. D'Arcy Power. *(Reprinted 1969.)* 45s.	1910
139 b, c, d, e, f,	*Extra Issue.* The Piers Plowman Controversy: *b.* Dr. Jusserand's 1st Reply to Prof. Manly; *c.* Prof. Manly's Answer to Dr. Jusserand; *d.* Dr. Jusserand's 2nd Reply to Prof. Manly; *e.* Mr. R. W. Chambers's Article; *f.* Dr. Henry Bradley's Rejoinder to Mr. R. W. Chambers. *(Out of print.)*	
140.	Capgrave's Lives of St. Augustine and St. Gilbert of Sempringham, ed. J. Munro. *(Out of print.)*	,,
E.S. 106.	Lydgate's Troy Book, ed. H. Bergen. Part III. *(Out of print.)*	,,
107.	Lydgate's Minor Poems, ed. H. N. MacCracken. Part I. Religious Poems. *(Reprinted 1961.)* 70s.	,,
O.S. 141.	Erthe upon Erthe, all the known texts, ed. Hilda Murray. *(Reprinted 1964.)* 30s.	1911
142.	The English Register of Godstow Nunnery, ed. A. Clark. Part III. 42s.	,,
143.	The Prose Life of Alexander, Thornton MSS., ed. J. S. Westlake. *(Out of print.)*	,,
E.S. 108.	Lydgate's Siege of Thebes, re-ed. A. Erdmann. Part I, the Text. *(Reprinted 1960.)* 50s.	,,
109.	Partonope, re-ed. A. T. Bödtker. The Texts. *(Out of print.)*	,,
O.S. 144.	The English Register of Oseney Abbey, by Oxford, ed. A. Clark. Part II. 20s.	1912
145.	The Northern Passion, ed. F. A. Foster. Part I, the four parallel texts. *(Out of print.)*	,,
E.S. 110.	Caxton's Mirrour of the World, with all the woodcuts, ed. O. H. Prior. *(Reprinted 1966.)* 50s.	,,
111.	Caxton's History of Jason, the Text, Part I, ed. J. Munro. *(Out of print.)*	,,
O.S. 146.	The Coventry Leet Book, ed. M. Dormer Harris. Introduction, Indexes, &c. Part IV. *(Out of print.)*	1913
147.	The Northern Passion, ed. F. A. Foster, Introduction, French Text, Variants and Fragments, Glossary. Part II. *(Out of print.)*	,,
	[An enlarged reprint of O.S. 26, Religious Pieces in Prose and Verse, from the Thornton MS., ed. G. G. Perry. *(Out of print.)*	
E.S. 112.	Lovelich's Romance of Merlin, ed. E. A. Kock. Part II. *(Reprinted 1961.)* 45s.	,,
113.	Poems by Sir John Salusbury, Robert Chester, and others, from Christ Church MS. 184, &c., ed. Carleton Brown. *(Out of print.)*	
O.S. 148.	A Fifteenth-Century Courtesy Book and Two Franciscan Rules, ed. R. W. Chambers and W. W. Seton. *(Reprinted 1963.)* 30s.	1914
149.	Lincoln Diocese Documents, 1450–1544, ed. Andrew Clark. *(Out of print.)*	,,
150.	The Old-English Rule of Bp. Chrodegang, and the Capitula of Bp. Theodulf, ed. A. S. Napier. *(Out of print.)*	
E.S. 114.	The Gild of St. Mary, Lichfield, ed. F. J. Furnivall. 27s.	,,
115.	The Chester Plays, re-ed. J. Matthews. Part II. *(Reprinted 1967.)* 38s.	,,
O.S. 151.	The Lanterne of Light, ed. Lilian M. Swinburn. *(Out of print.)*	1915
152.	Early English Homilies, from Cott. Vesp. D. XIV, ed. Rubie Warner. Part I, Text. *(Out of print.)*	,,
E.S. 116.	The Pauline Epistles, ed. M. J. Powell. *(Out of print.)*	,,
117.	Bp. Fisher's English Works, ed. R. Bayne. Part II. *(Out of print.)*	,,
O.S. 153.	Mandeville's Travels, ed. P. Hamelius. Part I, Text. *(Reprinted 1960.)* 40s.	1916
154.	Mandeville's Travels, ed. P. Hamelius. Part II, Notes and Introduction. *(Reprinted 1961.)* 40s.	,,
E.S. 118.	The Earliest Arithmetics in English, ed. R. Steele. *(Out of print.)*	,,
119.	The Owl and the Nightingale, 2 Texts parallel, ed. G. F. H. Sykes and J. H. G. Grattan. *(Out of print.)*	,,
O.S. 155.	The Wheatley MS., ed. Mabel Day. 54s.	1917
E.S. 120.	Ludus Coventriae, ed. K. S. Block. *(Reprinted 1961.)* 60s.	,,
O.S. 156.	Reginald Pecock's Donet, from Bodl. MS. 916, ed. Elsie V. Hitchcock. 63s.	1918
E.S. 121.	Lydgate's Fall of Princes, ed. H. Bergen. Part I. *(Reprinted 1967.)* 63s.	,,
122.	Lydgate's Fall of Princes, ed. H. Bergen. Part II. *(Reprinted 1967.)* 63s.	,,
O.S. 157.	Harmony of the Life of Christ, from MS. Pepys 2498, ed. Margery Goates. *(Out of print.)*	1919
158.	Meditations on the Life and Passion of Christ, from MS. Add., 11307, ed. Charlotte D'Evelyn. *(Out of print.)*	
E.S. 123.	Lydgate's Fall of Princes, ed. H. Bergen. Part III. *(Reprinted 1967.)* 63s.	,,
124.	Lydgate's Fall of Princes, ed. H. Bergen. Part IV. *(Reprinted 1967.)* 90s.	,,
O.S. 159.	Vices and Virtues, ed. F. Holthausen. Part II. *(Reprinted 1967.)* 28s.	1920
	[A re-edition of O.S. 18, Hali Meidenhad, ed. O. Cockayne, with a variant MS., Bodl. 34, hitherto unprinted, ed. F. J. Furnivall. *(Out of print.)*	,,
E.S. 125.	Lydgate's Siege of Thebes, ed. A. Erdmann and E. Ekwall. Part II. *(Out of print.)*	,,

E.S.	126. Lydgate's Troy Book, ed. H. Bergen. Part IV. (*Out of print*.)	1920
O.S.	160. The Old English Heptateuch, MS. Cott. Claud. B. IV, ed. S. J. Crawford. (*Reprinted* 1969.) 75s.	1921
	161. Three O.E. Prose Texts, MS. Cott. Vit. A. xv, ed. S. Rypins. (*Out of print*.)	,,
	162. Facsimile of MS. Cotton Nero A. x (Pearl, Cleanness, Patience and Sir Gawain), Introduction by I. Gollancz. (*Reprinted* 1955.) 200s.	1922
	163. Book of the Foundation of St. Bartholomew's Church in London, ed. N. Moore. (*Out of print*.)	1923
	164. Pecock's Folewer to the Donet, ed. Elsie V. Hitchcock. (*Out of print*.)	,,
	165. Middleton's Chinon of England, with Leland's Assertio Arturii and Robinson's translation, ed. W. E. Mead. (*Out of print*.)	,,
	166. Stanzaic Life of Christ, ed. Frances A. Foster. (*Out of print*.)	1924
	167. Trevisa's Dialogus inter Militem et Clericum, Sermon by FitzRalph, and Bygynnyng of the World, ed. A. J. Perry. (*Out of print*.)	,,
	168. Caxton's Ordre of Chyualry, ed. A. T. P. Byles. (*Out of print*.)	1925
	169. The Southern Passion, ed. Beatrice Brown. (*Out of print*.)	,,
	170. Walton's Boethius, ed. M. Science. (*Out of print*.)	,,
	171. Pecock's Reule of Cristen Religioun, ed. W. C. Greet. (*Out of print*.)	1926
	172. The Seege or Batayle of Troye, ed. M. E. Barnicle. (*Out of print*.)	,,
	173. Hawes' Pastime of Pleasure, ed. W. E. Mead. (*Out of print*.)	1927
	174. The Life of St. Anne, ed. R. E. Parker. (*Out of print*.)	,,
	175. Barclay's Eclogues, ed. Beatrice White. (*Reprinted* 1961.) 55s.	,,
	176. Caxton's Prologues and Epilogues, ed. W. J. B. Crotch. (*Reprinted* 1956.) 54s.	,,
	177. Byrhtferth's Manual, ed. S. J. Crawford. (*Reprinted* 1966.) 63s.	1928
	178. The Revelations of St. Birgitta, ed. W. P. Cumming. (*Out of print*.)	,,
	179. The Castell of Pleasure, ed. B. Cornelius. (*Out of print*.)	,,
	180. The Apologye of Syr Thomas More, ed. A. I. Taft. (*Out of print*.)	1929
	181. The Dance of Death, ed. F. Warren. (*Out of print*.)	,,
	182. Speculum Christiani, ed. G. Holmstedt. (*Out of print*.)	,,
	183. The Northern Passion (Supplement), ed. W. Heuser and Frances Foster. (*Out of print*.)	1930
	184. The Poems of John Audelay, ed. Ella K. Whiting. (*Out of print*.)	,,
	185. Lovelich's Merlin, ed. E. A. Kock. Part III. (*Out of print*.)	,,
	186. Harpsfield's Life of More, ed. Elsie V. Hitchcock and R. W. Chambers. (*Reprinted* 1963.) 105s.	1931
	187. Whittinton and Stanbridge's Vulgaria, ed. B. White. (*Out of print*.)	,,
	188. The Siege of Jerusalem, ed. E. Kölbing and Mabel Day. (*Out of print*.)	,,
	189. Caxton's Fayttes of Armes and of Chyualrye, ed. A. T. Byles. 63s.	1932
	190. English Mediæval Lapidaries, ed. Joan Evans and Mary Serjeantson. (*Reprinted* 1960.) 50s.	,,
	191. The Seven Sages, ed. K. Brunner. (*Out of print*.)	,,
	191A.On the Continuity of English Prose, by R. W. Chambers. (*Reprinted* 1966.) 25s.	,,
	192. Lydgate's Minor Poems, ed. H. N. MacCracken. Part II, Secular Poems. (*Reprinted* 1961.) 75s.	1933
	193. Seinte Marherete, re-ed. Frances Mack. (*Reprinted* 1958.) 50s.	,,
	194. The Exeter Book, Part II, ed. W. S. Mackie. (*Reprinted* 1938.) 42s.	,,
	195. The Quatrefoil of Love, ed. I. Gollancz and M. Weale. (*Out of print*.)	1934
	196. A Short English Metrical Chronicle, ed. E. Zettl. (*Out of print*.)	,,
	197. Roper's Life of More, ed. Elsie V. Hitchcock. (*Reprinted* 1958.) 35s.	,,
	198. Firumbras and Otuel and Roland, ed. Mary O'Sullivan. (*Out of print*.)	,,
	199. Mum and the Sothsegger, ed. Mabel Day and R. Steele. (*Out of print*.)	,,
	200. Speculum Sacerdotale, ed. E. H. Weatherly. (*Out of print*.)	1935
	201. Knyghthode and Bataile, ed. R. Dyboski and Z. M. Arend. (*Out of print*.)	,,
	202. Palsgrave's Acolastus, ed. P. L. Carver. (*Out of print*.)	,,
	203. Amis and Amiloun, ed. McEdward Leach. (*Reprinted* 1960.) 50s.	,,
	204. Valentine and Orson, ed. Arthur Dickson. (*Out of print*.)	1936
	205. Tales from the Decameron, ed. H. G. Wright. (*Out of print*.)	,,
	206. Bokenham's Lives of Holy Women (Lives of the Saints), ed. Mary S. Serjeantson. (*Out of print*.)	,,
	207. Liber de Diversis Medicinis, ed. Margaret S. Ogden. (*Out of print*.)	,,
	208. The Parker Chronicle and Laws (facsimile), ed. R. Flower and A. H. Smith. (*Out of print*.)	1937
	209. Middle English Sermons from MS. Roy. 18 B. xxiii, ed. W. O. Ross. (*Reprinted* 1960.) 75s.	1938
	210. Sir Gawain and the Green Knight, ed. I. Gollancz. With Introductory essays by Mabel Day and M. S. Serjeantson. (*Reprinted* 1966.) 25s.	,,
	211. Dictes and Sayings of the Philosophers, ed. C. F. Bühler. (*Reprinted* 1961.) 75s.	1939
	212. The Book of Margery Kempe, Part I, ed. S. B. Meech and Hope Emily Allen. (*Reprinted* 1961.) 70s.	,,
	213. Ælfric's De Temporibus Anni, ed. H. Henel. (*Out of print*.)	1940
	214. Morley's Translation of Boccaccio's De Claris Mulieribus, ed. H. G. Wright. (*Out of print*.)	,,
	215. English Poems of Charles of Orleans, Part I, ed. R. Steele. (*Out of print*.)	1941
	216. The Latin Text of the Ancrene Riwle, ed. Charlotte D'Evelyn. (*Reprinted* 1957.) 45s.	,,
	217. The Book of Vices and Virtues, ed. W. Nelson Francis. (*Reprinted* 1968.) 75s.	1942
	218. The Cloud of Unknowing and the Book of Privy Counselling, ed. Phyllis Hodgson. (*Reprinted* 1958.) 40s.	1943
	219. The French Text of the Ancrene Riwle, B.M. Cotton MS. Vitellius. F. VII, ed. J. A. Herbert. (*Reprinted* 1967.) 55s.	,,
	220. English Poems of Charles of Orleans, Part II, ed. R. Steele and Mabel Day. (*Out of print*.)	1944
	221. Sir Degrevant, ed. L. F. Casson. (*Out of print*.)	,,
	222. Ro. Ba.'s Life of Syr Thomas More, ed. Elsie V. Hitchcock and Mgr. P. E. Hallett. (*Reprinted* 1957.) 63s.	1945
	223. Tretyse of Loue, ed. J. H. Fisher. (*Out of print*.)	,,
	224. Athelston, ed. A. McI. Trounce. (*Reprinted* 1957.) 42s.	1946
	225. The English Text of the Ancrene Riwle, B.M. Cotton MS. Nero A. XIV, ed. Mabel Day. (*Reprinted* 1957.) 50s.	,,

226. Respublica, re-ed. W. W. Greg. (*Out of print*.)	1946
227. Kyng Alisaunder, ed. G. V. Smithers. Vol. I, Text. (*Reprinted* 1961.) 75*s*.	1947
228. The Metrical Life of St. Robert of Knaresborough, ed. J. Bazire. (*Reprinted* 1968.) 42*s*.	,,
229. The English Text of the Ancrene Riwle, Gonville and Caius College MS. 234/120, ed. R. M. Wilson. With Introduction by N. R. Ker. (*Reprinted* 1957.) 35*s*.	1948
230. The Life of St. George by Alexander Barclay, ed. W. Nelson. (*Reprinted* 1960.) 40*s*.	,,
231. Deonise Hid Diuinite, and other treatises related to *The Cloud of Unknowing*, ed. Phyllis Hodgson. (*Reprinted* 1958.) 50*s*.	1949
232. The English Text of the Ancrene Riwle, B.M. Royal MS. 8 C. 1, ed. A. C. Baugh. (*Reprinted* 1958.) 30*s*.	,,
233. The Bibliotheca Historica of Diodorus Siculus translated by John Skelton, ed. F. M. Salter and H. L. R. Edwards. Vol. I, Text. (*Reprinted* 1968.) 80*s*.	1950
234. Caxton: Paris and Vienne, ed. MacEdward Leach. (*Out of print*.)	1951
235. The South English Legendary, Corpus Christi College Cambridge MS. 145 and B.M. M.S. Harley 2277, &c., ed. Charlotte D'Evelyn and Anna J. Mill. Text, Vol. I. (*Reprinted* 1967.) 63*s*.	,,
236. The South English Legendary. Text, Vol. II. (*Reprinted* 1967.) 63*s*.	1952
[E.S. 87. Two Coventry Corpus Christi Plays, re-ed. H. Craig. Second Edition. (*Reprinted* 1967.) 30*s*.]	,,
237. Kyng Alisaunder, ed. G. V. Smithers. Vol. II, Introduction, Commentary, and Glossary. 50*s*.	1953
238. The Phonetic Writings of Robert Robinson, ed. E. J. Dobson. (*Reprinted* 1968.) 30*s*.	,,
239. The Bibliotheca Historica of Diodorus Siculus translated by John Skelton, ed. F. M. Salter and H. L. R. Edwards. Vol. II. Introduction, Notes, and Glossary. 30*s*.	1954
240. The French Text of the Ancrene Riwle, Trinity College, Cambridge, MS. R. 14, 7, ed. W. H. Trethewey. 55*s*.	,,
241. Þe Wohunge of ure Lauerd, and other pieces, ed. W. Meredith Thompson. 45*s*.	1955
242. The Salisbury Psalter, ed. Celia Sisam and Kenneth Sisam. (*Reprinted* 1969.) 90*s*.	1955–56
243. George Cavendish: The Life and Death of Cardinal Wolsey, ed. Richard S. Sylvester. (*Reprinted* 1961.) 45*s*.	1957
244. The South English Legendary. Vol. III, Introduction and Glossary, ed. C. D'Evelyn. 30*s*.	,,
245. Beowulf (facsimile). With Transliteration by J. Zupitza, new collotype plates, and Introduction by N. Davis. (*Reprinted* 1967.) 100*s*.	1958
246. The Parlement of the Thre Ages, ed. M. Y. Offord. (*Reprinted* 1967.) 40*s*.	1959
247. Facsimile of MS. Bodley 34 (Katherine Group). With Introduction by N. R. Ker. 63*s*.	,,
248. Þe Liflade ant te Passiun of Seinte Iuliene, ed. S. R. T. O. d'Ardenne. 40*s*.	1960
249. Ancrene Wisse, Corpus Christi College, Cambridge, MS. 402, ed. J. R. R. Tolkien. With an Introduction by N. R. Ker. 50*s*.	,,
250. Laȝamon's Brut, ed. G. L. Brook and R. F. Leslie. Vol. I, Text (first part). 100*s*.	1961
251. Facsimile of the Cotton and Jesus Manuscripts of the Owl and the Nightingale. With Introduction by N. R. Ker. 50*s*.	1962
252. The English Text of the Ancrene Riwle, B.M. Cotton MS. Titus D. xviii, ed. Frances M. Mack, and Lanhydrock Fragment, ed. A. Zettersten. 50*s*.	,,
253. The Bodley Version of Mandeville's Travels, ed. M. C. Seymour. 50*s*.	1963
254. Ywain and Gawain, ed. Albert B. Friedman and Norman T. Harrington. 50*s*.	,,
255. Facsimile of B.M. MS. Harley 2253 (The Harley Lyrics). With Introduction by N. R. Ker. 100*s*.	1964
256. Sir Eglamour of Artois, ed. Frances E. Richardson. 50*s*.	1965
257. Sir Thomas Chaloner: The Praise of Folie, ed. Clarence H. Miller. 50*s*.	,,
258. The Orchard of Syon, ed. Phyllis Hodgson and Gabriel M. Liegey. Vol. I, Text. 100*s*.	1966
259. Homilies of Ælfric: A Supplementary Collection, ed. J. C. Pope. Vol. I. 100*s*.	1967
260. Homilies of Ælfric: A Supplementary Collection, ed. J. C. Pope. Vol. II. 100*s*.	1968
261. Lybeaus Desconus, ed. M. Mills. 50*s*.	1969
262. The Macro Plays, re-ed. Mark Eccles. 50*s*.	,,

Forthcoming volumes

263. Caxton's History of Reynard the Fox, ed. N. F. Blake. (*At press*.) 50*s*.	1970
264. Scrope's Epistle of Othea, ed. C. F. Bühler. (*At press*.) 50*s*.	,,
265. The Cyrurgie of Guy de Chauliac, ed. Margaret S. Ogden. Vol. I, Text. (*At Press*.) 100*s*.	1971
266. Wulfstan's Canons of Edgar, ed. R. G. Fowler. (*At press*.) 50*s*.	1972
267. The English Text of the Ancrene Riwle, B. M. Cotton MS. Cleopatra C. vi, ed. E. J. Dobson. (*At press*.) 50*s*.	,,

Other texts are in preparation.

Supplementary Texts

The Society proposes to issue some Supplementary Texts from time to time as funds allow. These will be sent to members as part of the normal issue and will also be available to non-members at listed prices. The first of these, Supplementary Text 1, expected to appear in 1970, will be *Non-Cycle Plays and Fragments*, ed. Norman Davis (about 50*s*.). This is a completely revised and re-set edition of the texts in Extra Series 104 with some additional pieces. Supplementary Text 2, expected to appear in 1971, will be *Caxton's Knight of La Tour Landry*, ed. M. Y. Offord (at press, about 50*s*.).

April 1969

The manufacturer's authorised representative in the EU for product safety is Oxford University Press España S.A. of El Parque Empresarial San Fernando de Henares, Avenida de Castilla, 2 - 28830 Madrid (www.oup.es/en or product.safety@oup.com). OUP España S.A. also acts as importer into Spain of products made by the manufacturer.
Printed and bound by CPI Group (UK) Ltd, Croydon, CR0 4YY

23/03/2026

02076308-0004